I have known Mike DeLucia most of n[illegible],
his coach, his director, his colleague, but most of all ... his *friend.*

If I had to describe Mike in one word that word would be *passionate.* Mike never gives less than 110% to anything that he considers to be *important.* Whether it was in the classroom, on the baseball field, on the stage, or in his role as a parent, Mike is what we all commonly refer to as *dedicated.*

So when Mike told me that he was separating himself from one of the true "loves of his life," the New York Yankees, to write a book on how to fix what he feels is destroying both our national pastime and our beloved "Bronx Bombers," I knew that Mike's patience with the game he cherishes had reached a *boiling point.*

Mike has written a book that will make you harken back to a time when the game seemed to be "larger than life." However, tread lightly, because with every *nostalgic* step.you take you will find yourself becoming more and more annoyed with what the game we all loved has become both on and off the field.

As a fellow "lifelong" Yankees fan, I can attest to the fact that this book will make you smile, it will make you nod your head in agreement, it will make you scream, and you may even find yourself throwing the book across the room. Mike does not treat our heroes as "sacred cows." He treats them as talented, gifted athletes, who have to answer for their decisions, statements, and choices. He doesn't put them on a shelf and worship them from afar. He holds them accountable for what they and the "game" have become.

While you may not agree with everything that Mike has to say, he *will* make you think and in the process temper your inclination to become one more "unthinking cog" in the *corporate machine.*

At a time in our country when everyone is asking "why all the wealth is in the hands of a select few," Mike provides us with some *insight.* Unfortunately, in the process, he offers us a *scathing critique* of some of our most "beloved" players, our front office, our team, our league, and our once *beautiful game.* A game which has been ripped out of the hands of the fans and rests tightly in the clutches of a few of baseball's ironfisted overlords.

BOYCOTT THE YANKEES is not a book for the faint of heart. It is a clarion call to arms for the fans of the Yankees and the fans of baseball to do something before the game we know and love is gone *forever.*

Ron MacFarland

"Greed keeps men forever poor, even the abundance of this world will not make them rich."

~ Mongolian Proverb

A first grade teacher explains to her class that she is a Boston Red Sox fan. She asks her students to raise their hands if they were Red Sox fans, too. Not really knowing what a Red Sox fan was, but wanting to be like their teacher, hands explode into the air like flashy fireworks. There is, however, one exception. A girl named Lucy has not gone along with the crowd. The teacher asks her why she has decided to be different. "Because I'm not a Red Sox fan." "Then," asks the teacher, "What are you?" "Why I'm proud to be a Yankees fan," boasts the little girl. The teacher is a little perturbed now; her face slightly red. She asks Lucy why she is a Yankees fan. "Well, my dad and mom are Yankees fans, and I'm a Yankees fan, too!" The teacher is now angry. "That's no reason," she says loudly. "What if your mom was a moron, and your dad was a moron. What would you be then?" A pause, and a smile. "Then," says Lucy, "I'd be a Red Sox fan."

Boycott The Yankees

Hi Trish,
Enjoy the book!

Boycott The Yankees

A Call to Action by a Lifelong Yankees Fan

Mike DeLucia

Green-T Books
New York

ISBN-13: 9780997174106
ISBN-10: 0997174102
Library of Congress Control Number: 2016900660
Green-T-Books, Somers, NY

Dedicated to my father, Joe DeLucia, the man who fostered both my love of baseball and my love of the New York Yankees.

. . . .

Editor: Elizabeth Lewis

. . . .

Illustrations: Richard Wiley

. . . .

Photography: Jamie Gouger

. . . .

With thanks to
Ron MacFarland

Introductions Are Entirely Necessary

• • •

It makes me sick, and it breaks my heart—it really does, and I'm angry! The *it* to which I'm referring cannot be summed up in a few pointed phrases because it covers a lot of territory—a whole book's worth, actually. Being a high school English teacher, I understand the nebulous nature of indefinite pronoun it, and I tell my students to avoid the word whenever possible as it can confuse the reader. In order to explain *its* meaning, I'll be discussing, haranguing, and debating two separate yet connected areas that are dear to my heart: baseball and the New York Yankees—two entities that go back to my earliest memories.

Baseball, or some version of it, was the prevailing theme of my youth, and the living spirit of the Yankees was within me as I competed on the streets, parks, and empty lots of the Bronx. There was a subconscious connection between baseball and my prideful identity as a New York Yankees fan. I didn't play baseball because of the Yankees—I loved baseball, but I loved baseball better because of my allegiance to the Bombers. So my inspiration for this book grew from the fervent core of both my distant and not-so-distant past. Twenty years ago, I could never have imagined that I would one day write a book calling for a boycott of the New York Yankees. Writing those words is uncomfortable for me because they sound blasphemous.

How does an *individual* born and raised in the Bronx—a *child* who navigated the world of the 1960's and 1970's, played little league (imagining himself as Mickey Mantle when he stepped up to the plate)—a *boy* who learned about the Bronx Bombers, the historic, magnificent, one and only New York Yankees from his father—a *kid* who grew up trading, flipping, and scaling baseball cards, who relished the prized yellow-toned Louisville Sluggers given out on Bat Day at Yankee Stadium—a *youngster* who argued with despicable New York Mets fans about who was the better team in 1969 when the Mets owned the World Series trophy and the Yankees owned fifth-place in the newly created American League East (28½ games behind the first place Baltimore Orioles who were beaten by the Mets in '69)—a *teenager* who followed the Yankees from the horrific CBS years through the turbulent and exciting General Von Steingrabber era—a *guy* who followed each game, either on radio or television, and then read about it in the newspaper the following morning—a *man* who went to Yankees.com every day of the off-season to see what was going on in the world of the Bronx Bombers—a *devoted fan* who proudly purchased Yankees hats, T-shirts, jackets, books, films, and banners for myself, family, and friends—a *father* who continued the revered family tradition of raising his son to be a Yankees fan—

—to a *person* who rarely watches or listens to games and resists the instinctive urge to flip over the newspaper so I may read lofty praise or biting criticism about the Yankees' present state of affairs?

I didn't arrive at this place because the dynasty collapsed or because I've lost interest in baseball. This unexpected, unforeseen outcome developed from the complexity of the *it* that makes me sick, angry, and brokenhearted. As you read these pages you may find that the plurality of feelings behind this pronoun is a shared experience for both of us. And like most people reading this book, I didn't study sports journalism in college, go to sports broadcasting school, or play pro ball… I'm a fan. My credentials were developed over a lifetime of rooting for the Yankees, reading about them, watching them, talking about them, and even dreaming about them after watching the Bombers on TV before going to bed—especially late when they played on the west coast or in any series involving the Red Sox. While our specific histories and opinions may vary, you and I share a common ground and have been led to the same place. This book provides a means to an end, as it will reveal a solid plan to take back our team.

I'm certain that I'll be able to initiate change because something compelled you to pick up this book, and it's the same something that compelled me to write it—we're damned tired of what's happened to America's favorite pastime and are ready to take a stand against the billion dollar corporation hiding behind the beloved pinstripes and calling itself the New York Yankees.

PART 1

Biting the Hand That Feeds You

• • •

"There is a battle of two wolves inside us. One is evil. It is anger, jealousy, greed, resentment, lies, inferiority, and ego. The other is good. It is joy, peace, love, hope humility, kindness, empathy, and truth. The wolf that wins is the one you feed."

~ Native American Proverb, Cherokee

• • •

The Wonder Years

Before I explain why I have separated myself from the New York Yankees, it's relevant that you know something about my history. I was born and raised in the Bronx, New York, and the Yankees, whether it be by image, concept, or name, have left an indelible mark on my psyche. Like summertime, family New Year's Eve parties, or my first friends, the Yankees were always there—no beginning that I can recall, as it resides in that area of the brain where memories seem to coincide with consciousness. As far as I know, I was always a Yankees fan, which makes the Yankees' arrogant betrayal of their fans *personal* for me.

The owners and players love to make statements such as "It's all for the fans," "The fans are what it's all about," or "Yankees fans are the best fans in the world," but this is one huge, shrewd, well-played load of BS! The Yankees spew that malarkey—that political-sounding propaganda, to stroke their own egos. Such statements make them look as though they actually care about us, and that, my Yankee *compadres*, is nothing but a lie. And in delivering this lie, they are mocking us. The cold reality is that the Yankees care little about fans. They mostly care about one thing—the bottom line, the end result, and to say it plainly… cash, as they are possessed by insatiable greed.

Many businesses, families, and individuals are concerned with the bottom line because they *must* be in order to stay afloat; however, the Yankees organization, worth $2.5 billion, is the most valuable sports team in America. Besides the obvious income streams derived from media contracts and game-day profits, the Yankees reap the rewards of renting out the stadium to superstar performers like Madonna, The Pinstripe Bowl (an NCAA division college football game), and the New York City Football Club (a soccer team that plays its home games at Yankee Stadium). Even *you* can rent out Yankee Stadium to take pictures: $1,500 during the week and $2000 on the weekend. Aside from these profits, the Yankees make millions annually from Major League Baseball Advanced Media or MLBAM (the interactive media and Internet company of Major League Baseball, which draws over four million hits daily), and these are just a few thin layers of their swollen financial juggernaut. I am not opposed to capitalism—on the contrary, I embrace capitalistic enterprise. I am, however, opposed to excessive greed on the corporate level at the expense of the average Joe. I'm all for the Yankees' continued mega-profits, and there's no reason to believe this ocean will dry up. So the Yankees must stop scamming their fans who work damned hard to put food on the table, to put their kids through college, and to put a few pennies away for retirement—ordinary people who must be concerned with the bottom line every single day of their lives. The Yankees will continue squeezing us until we speak up and show them that we are the heart of the Yankees' body, and if the heart stops beating, the body has a serious problem.

When talking about the Yankees, we say things like "We just got Masahiro Tanaka" or "We won last night" or "We lost last night." I still catch myself doing it at times because I still love the team, but the reality is that there is no *we*; it's an illusion we fans have created. Our role is to supply the organization with its financial resources and to cheer; but make no mistake about it—there is no *we*.

If this book touches a chord with enough people, I believe we will be part of the Yankees' scheme; there will be a *we*. The fans, not the corporations, are where the rubber meets the road. A shrinking fan base means shrinking dollars. If we're not going to games, watching them on cable, or paying obscene prices for merchandise, they will lose advertising dollars, and their empire will crumble. The gap between the Steinbrenners, the players, and the fans is wide and growing wider. Players and owners have all but taken fans out of the picture, except for when they are playing politics and spreading perfectly choreographed lies through the written word, the camera's eye, or the mouths of sports radio stations.

We will get the Yankees' attention if we are loyal to our cause. This book does not include impractical ideas such as buying the Steinbrenners' controlling shares of the team, yet our money will be the root of what may persuade the Yankees to consider us while brainstorming future plans regarding their magnificent empire—an empire which happens to be built upon the wallets of their humble fans. We deserve to be considered and not merely counted upon to feed the money machine's voracious appetite.

Don't you feel exploited bringing your family to a Yankees game? Just parking your car costs around $40.00. And besides parking you get hammered by food, ticket, and souvenir prices—you blow half your paycheck bringing your kids to a game! Haven't you vented your frustrations to others? If you haven't, you can't tell me you're satisfied with what's going on. You've been feeling this way because you and I were cut from the same cloth—we're Yankees fans—and because of this, I'm sure you'll be able to relate to my past. I figure if we're going to work together, you should know a little bit about me.

The Good Ole Days

It's said that you eventually turn into your parents, but when I was growing up I was convinced that would never happen to me, yet the older I get the more I hear myself say what my father often said: "It was *so* much better when I was a kid." Growing up in the Throgs Neck/Pelham Bay section of the Bronx in the '60s and '70s was special, and those times—our way of life, our innocence, our respect, our values, our society—have all but faded away. Play dates? You always had a play date because growing up in the Bronx meant every time you walked out the door you played with whomever was out there or *whoever* if I want to show off my Bronx grammar. Another popular New York regionalism from my era was using the plural form of second person "you," as in "Where *yous* going?" Being an

English teacher, my days of using the old lingo are long gone, but I have to admit that I sometimes subconsciously slip back into it if I'm around old friends.

Anyway, there was always a group of kids playing stickball, handball, stoop ball, Wiffleball (sewer to sewer), softball, off-the-wall, single-double-triple, skully, hopscotch, Johnny-on-the- pony, manhunt, tag, freeze tag, box tag (played using the squares on cement sidewalks), or red light-green light, and there were only a few props required for most of these games: a Spaldeen, a broomstick, a bottle cap and melted crayons, pieces of rock, or the requisite bat, ball, and glove. There were no cell phones and we weren't implanted with a computer chip so our mothers knew where we were. Your mother figured you were in the neighborhood because if you weren't you'd get a butt whooping, be punished, or both. We ate Chuckles, Necco candy wafers (I liked the black ones), Bit-O-Honey, Chick-O-Stick, Milk Duds, Charleston Chews, Peanut Chews, Good & Plenty and Good 'n Fruity, French burnt peanuts, Laffy Taffy, Circus Peanuts, candy cigarettes, Mallow Cups (you'd get that coin printed on the inside card so you could send away for a prize after you accumulated hundreds of them), Junior Mints, Razzles, Wax Lips, Gold Rocks Nugget Bubble Gum, Fruit Stripe Gum, Pez, chocolate gold coins, candy "button" dots on a white paper strip, licorice and strawberry laces (two for a penny at Jennings candy store on Tremont Avenue across from Frank Bee), homemade Italian ice, and the best cookies, pastries, and pizza in the country. We drank chocolate, vanilla, cherry, and lemon-lime fountain sodas from soda shops that made egg creams, milk shakes, ice cream sodas, and root beer floats. We also drank water straight from garden hoses, and it tasted awesome on a hot day. We opened *Johnny Pumps* (fire hydrants) in the summer and had a blast, literally, and managed to survive and thrive without hand sanitizer and goofy looking bicycle helmets. If you wore a bicycle helmet back then, the harassment would have hurt worse than the potential head injury. I mean, aren't bicycle helmets the goofiest looking apparel ever created? Who thought up that ridiculous design?

One of the highlights of summertime was going to Jones Beach. We'd get up at 6:00 a.m., make sandwiches, iced tea, and snacks—remember those Mr. Salty pretzels in the box? My father would pack as many people as possible into our Dodge station wagon and then we made the long drive to Wantagh, Long Island. Once there, we'd take out the *thousand* pound cooler, beach chairs, and all the other paraphernalia and hike, what seemed like miles, to the boardwalk. We'd make the long trek over the scorching hot, fine white sand to the sounds of seagulls, crashing waves, and the smell of salt water. Once Mom and Dad chose the *right* spot, we'd run into the cold ocean and have the time of our lives riding waves and eating sandy sandwiches. What was with that warm spot in the ocean? My brother would say it was fish pee. After lunch our parents wouldn't let us go in the water until we waited thirty minutes. We'd sit there staring at the ocean and frequently annoy them by asking how many minutes had passed. Thirty minutes felt like three hours.

Most of the time we'd stay at Jones Beach until the crowd thinned, and we'd feed seagulls with leftover pieces of dinner sandwiches, potato salad, and Wise potato chips or Cheese Doodles. Right before you went home, your mom would hold the towel around you so you could change out of your bathing suit only to have an older sibling try to rip it away while you were standing there buck naked on the beach. The ride home was the *worst* because you had sand everywhere, your hair was plastered to your head, you felt grimy from the salt water, and you had to squeeze into the sweltering car and sit on those blisteringly hot vinyl seats for the long ride home. That was when you wished you'd taken your mother's advice and washed off the saltwater under the cold, freshwater showers near the boardwalk. We didn't have an air conditioner in our car back then, so all the windows were rolled down while we inched through Long Island traffic. However, the car turned into a wind tunnel when the road opened up and Dad drove back home at full speed. You could still feel the waves when you got into bed at night, and you slept well because you were exhausted from all that fun.

In 1973, my father drove us across the country just prior to the energy crisis; gas was about 35¢ a gallon. We drove from New York to California to visit my aunt Anna who had just moved there after Sinclair (Remember Sinclair gas stations with the big green brontosaurus logo?) moved their offices to the west coast. While many people had car air conditioning in '73, the DeLucias did not, so we drove across the country with five people in a 1970 Oldsmobile Cutlass Supreme. That was like one really, really long ride back from Jones Beach; yet, it was fun. I have a lot of special memories from that trip—sweaty, hot, wind-tunnel driving and all.

Things were simpler back then too. As society evolves it produces devices intended to make life simpler, yet life is much more complex now. We grew up in a time when there was one house phone and maybe an extension where you would try to listen in on other people's conversations. A busy signal would sound if someone from the house you were calling was on the phone, and you had to wait, sometimes hours, until the line was free. Call waiting and then cell phones obliterated that "inconvenience." Now instead of waiting to call someone back, we are always available, married to phones, and in a way, we've moved further away from each other.

The home computer, a necessary part of our world, makes so many things easy and convenient (remember looking words up in a dictionary or using an encyclopedia?), but there's no question that life was better without it. We interacted with each other. We dealt with our issues in real time. Dealing with people in person is a lot less destructive than bashing them on social media. We didn't rely on another person's imagination through computer animation and/or video game graphics. The computer euthanized the average kid's imagination and sense of discovery. We didn't play computer games over the Internet with our friends who were secluded in their rooms; we played with each other in the same space, live! We built things: wagons, forts, bikes, rafts. I loved building wagons with my friends. We'd get a set of wheels off an old baby carriage and with some wood, nails, cotter pins, rope, and a wood milk box we'd be racing down a hill in a cart we built that day. And men were men, women were women, and kids were kids back then. It was far from perfect, but there's something to be said for that traditional mindset. We knew our roles. Mom had dinner on the table every night and we all ate as a family. There was a dinner time, and there were consequences if you were late. And our parents were our parents—not our friends. Our parents became our friends once we were adults.

Life was so much more formal in those days. I remember when my aunt Anna took us to see *Grease* on Broadway (I was annoyed because I thought it was going to be a "boring" play about ancient Greece), and we went dressed in our best clothes. Today people attend Broadway shows with the same clothes they wear to the mall. That was another thing—we didn't have malls in the Bronx. There was one mall in New Rochelle, a thirty-minute drive from my house, but it was small in comparison to the monster malls of today; it didn't even have a food court. Everything was smaller in those days. Our homes were much smaller too. Houses have gotten huge over the years. My mother, father, two brothers, and I (along with my Uncle Joe who lived downstairs, but was usually in our apartment), lived in a four-room apartment with one bathroom. We also had three boys in one bedroom—the same room as the family phone, which always seemed to ring at the crack of dawn on weekends.

Things were certainly different back then, and a vital part of our lives was baseball. Not the kind the kids play today with all the pressure, designer uniforms, and bats that cost $300. Many kids didn't have their own bats, but we'd share whatever equipment we had. We even shared gloves with the opposing team, because we'd sometimes have to gather kids hanging around the park just to have enough guys to play. Between innings, gloves would be tossed around from kid to kid. Sometimes there'd be a left-handed kid playing the field with a right-handed glove, because all of the other gloves were taken. My brothers and I had new bats every year simply because we went to Bat Day at Yankee Stadium. I see kids walking into my classroom with an enormous bag packed with baseball gear. It puzzles me because we didn't need a bag. We slid our glove over our wood bat handle, put it over our shoulder, and walked to the park hobo style—hopefully someone remembered the ball. Sometimes we didn't have a ball and we'd search the neighborhood for soda cans or (glass) bottles, which often included looking through public trash bins. Finding a 7-Up bottle was a score because we got 7¢ for those! It would take half a day to find enough bottles to pay for a ball. Do you remember playing baseball or softball with a waterlogged ball that couldn't go out of the infield even if you hit it on the sweet spot with everything you had or baseballs held together with electric tape as a cover? Sometimes we played with a baseball that had no cover or tape, and it would unwind as the game went on. You'd hit the ball and it had strings trailing like a comet.

Baseball was one of the ways we learned about life. People use baseball metaphors to describe life because the game holds life's lessons within its framework. You must learn to negotiate, interrogate, persuade. One must sacrifice, and learn that you don't have to hit a home run every time; and while having two strikes against you is uncomfortable, there's not a feeling in the world that compares to knocking it out of the park after you're behind in the count. No one ever likes to be caught off-base, and getting to first base is essential, playing hardball is sometimes necessary, crowding the plate might cause a confrontation, and as the great Yogi put it, "It ain't over till it's over." While I played other sports, I was only loyal to the Yankees. I cared if the Knicks or Nets, Giants or Jets, or Rangers or Islanders were playing for the championship, but I didn't think too much about it; I hardly knew the players. Baseball was it for me, and the Yankees were the center of that sacred world.

Baseball cards were an essential part of the Bronx childhood (Remember that powdered gum stick that shattered like glass?), and it wasn't about saving the cards to sell at some point in the future; we cherished baseball cards for their emotional and social value. It was about scaling or flipping them to win a Mel Stottlemyre, Fritz Peterson, or Joe Pepitone when all you had were a bunch of scrubs or doubles. If you didn't scale the scrubs, doubles, or Mets cards, you would clothespin them to your bike frame so they would *slap* against the wheel spokes when you pedaled, and that sound turned your bicycle into a "motorcycle." Going to school with a few cards and ending up with a whole stack made a boy proud, and losing your prized possessions stung as badly as catching a beating from one of the nuns at St. Benedict's Grammar School. We would memorize players' statistics better than our schoolwork. The men on those cards were our gods, and we worshipped them on the hallowed grounds of Yankee Stadium as well as any other baseball park we played on. We wanted to be them.

I remember signing up for the Pelham Bay Little League year after year. First you registered and paid your fee and then you were given *chances* (raffles) to sell, which your parents wound up buying. We always waited until the night before they were due to start filling out all those stubs. I remember anxiously waiting for my coach to call and tell me what team I would be on and what time to meet for the first practice. We didn't have travel teams, so the games were all located in the neighborhood. We played at Pelham Bay Park, The Indian Museum field, or at Wilkinson Park—a park that was very close to the first Son of Sam shooting. If I didn't walk to games as I mentioned earlier, I rode my Schwinn Sting-Ray Chopper to the field with my glove hanging from the left side of my ape-hanger handlebars, because the right side had the brake; extra bats were supplied by the league. If I happened to win a game, I would imitate the Scooter, announcing my heroics with a "Holy Cow!" as I relived my big hit, diving catch, or game-winning-dust-cloud slide into home plate.

Three Die Hard Generations

Going to Yankee Stadium was a family tradition. We looked forward to Bat Day the most, because it was thrilling getting a free bat autographed by one of the Yankees. We were so excited to see which of our heroes' signatures would be scripted on the barrel. I remember my Mickey Mantle, Roy White, Joe Pepitone, Tom Tresh, Bobby Murcer, Horace Clarke, and Thurman Munson bats. I know I had more but they're long gone. While in the stands at Bat Day, we would put a used soda cup on the barrel of the bat and smash it into the floor vertically to create an explosive *pop*. After we used up all of our cups, we would look for any discarded ones lying around. Germs? Who cared about germs?

The Yankees were some of the threads woven into our family fabric; we were Yankees fans and damned proud of it. Back then, and up until my recent separation, it was like the Yankees players were a part of our extended family. We knew about their families, their stats, their injuries, and their best and worst performances. We all cried when Thurman died. We cried with Reggie, and Billy, and again when Murcer won the game that night, and when we read Bill Gallo's cartoon with Thurman's face, eyes closed, looking down from the heavens as Yuchie and his friend, with bowed heads and tears rolling off their cheeks, walked away from home plate because they couldn't bring themselves to play ball that day. We felt the ecstasy of our Yankees' triumphs when they surged in the 1970s and again during the dynasty of the 90s and early 2000s. In 2004 we experienced legitimate pain while watching the Boston Red Sox celebrating on the field at Yankee Stadium when they beat us in that infamous, unforgettable, gut-wrenching series. My family and friends talked about the Yankees; we argued about the Yankees; and we cheered the Yankees on through their victories—and victories were rare during the dark days of CBS ownership. No Yankees fan during this era could forget 1969 when the Mets were World Series champs and we had to eat crow for nearly ten years.

My father, Joe DeLucia, was the first DeLucia Yankees fan. My grandfather, Alfredo, immigrated to this country from Italy during the depression, and his priority was putting food on the table. My father found the Yankees on his own. Dad played baseball with his friends now and again, but he often worked with my grandfather after school and on weekends. My grandfather used to sell crystalline (bleach), door-to-door. After making the crystalline from a purchased concentrate, they'd bottle it (in used wine gallons), and distribute it all over the Fordham section of the Bronx; there wasn't much time for play. My dad's friends were Yankees fans, but since my father had never been to Yankee Stadium, he didn't have the connection, and anyone who's ever had the privilege of experiencing the Cathedral of Baseball understands the lure of that place—I really do miss it. But anyway, one day while Dad was listening to the radio, he came across a Yankees game. They were losing by five or six runs and the opposing team was at bat, so Dad flipped the dial and listened to music for about an hour. He later returned to see how the Yankees were doing, and he heard sounds of cheering fans; Joe DiMaggio won the game in the bottom of the ninth inning. From that moment on, he became a bona fide Yankees fan. Going to the ballpark and watching them live intensified his allegiance.

My brothers and I carried that tradition on with our children. My son, Michael, was born in 1987, and the early eighties were dark years for the Yankees because of all the Steinbrenner buffoonery. When my son was five or six, he said, "Dad, I want to be a Toronto Blue Jays fan." I replied, "Michael, you have the right to follow any baseball team you choose, but if it's not the Yankees, you have to sleep in the yard." That was the end of that! The Yankees tradition became a powerful bond between my son and me. Even though the beginning of my son's exposure to the Yankees was tough, he was born at the perfect time because the Yankees began to click in 1994. A few months after the Yankees won in 2009, my son and I made a pact that we would get matching Yankees tattoos after their twenty-eighth championship. We are not tattoo people, but we would make an exception, as this would be a symbol of our mutual love and respect for each other and our team. Sadly, that's one pact I would not be able to honor if the Yankees were to win their twenty-eighth title this year.

PART 2

Poor Man, Rich Man

• • •

"No matter how full the river, it still wants to grow."

~ Congolese Proverb

• • •

The Reserve Clause

Modern-day baseball fans react incredulously when they learn that many major league players had to work during the off season just to make ends meet, and that these professional athletes were required to serve their country (a minimum of two years usually during their prime), and got paid the standard armed forces salary of roughly $68.00 per week. Even after the advent of free agency, many players worked because few were guaranteed contracts beyond one year. Pro baseball players worked as salesmen, farmhands, singers, gas pumpers, pharmacists, ranchers, miners, delivery men, college-team coaches, manufacturers, and various other middle class occupations. Richard "The Gravedigger" Hebner, who played for the Mets in 1979, earned that nickname because he dug graves during the off season. Even Yankees legends Yogi Berra and Phil Rizzuto after winning the 1951 World Series sold suits together at a store in New Jersey to supplement their income. Can you imagine walking into a men's store and have salesmen Yogi Berra and Phil Rizzuto helping you pick out a suit and then one of them ringing you up at the cash register?

Making it to the World Series meant more to the ballplayers of yesteryear than it does to the lavish, self-indulgent, outrageously overpaid *prima donnas* of today. While the bliss and glory of a grueling World Series accomplishment is a shared experience among baseball ballplayers of any era, the pros of the past were also fighting for financial stability. In 1973 the average major leaguer's salary was approximately $36,500 and the winning World Series share per player was approximately $24,600, a bonus of over sixty-five percent. In 2015, the average pro baseball salary is approximately $4.25 million and the World Series cut is roughly $350,000. For many established ballplayers, World Series money is, in a way, a pay cut. The World Series paycheck was an important bargaining chip for the Yankees in the days before free agency. As a team who frequented the postseason, the Yankees had been able to make dissatisfied players an offer that was hard for them to refuse. Players could either submit to the organization's contractual demands or chance losing their accustomed championship bonus; many signed and fought hard for that money.

Joltin' Joe DiMaggio challenged Yankees owner Colonel Jacob Ruppert during heated contract negotiations. The Yankees offered DiMaggio $17,000 and he countered with $40,000. Yankees business manager Ed Barrow argued that $40,000 exceeded what they paid the great Lou Gehrig. Joe D responded by telling Mr. Barrow that Lou Gehrig was greatly underpaid. Eventually, DiMaggio reluctantly accepted the Yankees' final offer of $25,000 for only one reason—he was virtually powerless. With the reserve clause, owners were like kings; they owned the team, which included the players on that team. A ballplayer was bound to the team who signed him for the rest of his playing days, and the reserve clause provided owners with this *divine* power for nearly one hundred years (1879-1975). Owners could sell, trade, or fire their players at will; they owned an individual's right to play pro baseball—and here's the kicker—the team owned an individual's rights to play ball even after his contract expired. If a retired player wanted to play again, his owner decided whether he could or not.

Was there animosity? You bet there was, and you'd be hard pressed to find anyone outside of an owner who would say the animosity wasn't justified. The Chicago Black Sox scandal proves this. No organization or individual should have the right to hold that kind of power over another person's life; it's an injustice, and it creates hostility. The peace of World War I engendered World War II, and the reserve clause, with its inequitable structure, created the hubristic ball players of today. Owners created that monster and fans are literally paying the price. Teams now *have* to pay exorbitant amounts of money for slightly above average ballplayers. A player who bats in the .280 range can demand 10 to 15 million dollars a year. Thirty-seven year old MLB drifter Carlos Beltran signed a three year $45 million contract with the Yankees. He was guaranteed $15 million a year, even if his average were to drop to, let's say, .230, which it did during his first year with the Bombers. Can you imagine batting .230 and making $15 million for your services?

However, owners aren't going to let that dilemma stand in the way of their greed; they'll just raise prices, because they know that fans will remain loyal—cost will not dissuade fans from loving their team! Fans are the ones who want their children to have that sacred Yankees Jersey, glove, bat, hat, or banner. How do we refuse our children the excitement of seeing their heroes at Yankee Stadium? The average U.S. household's credit-card debt is over $15,000, but you continue to struggle through and buy these things for your family because it's embarrassing when you have to tell your kids you can't afford to buy them a ticket to a game or buy them Yankees apparel. Parents stress over taking their family to a game, while Alex Rodriguez wipes sweat from his brow with $100 bills—and that's not a metaphor; A-Rod actually did that while having lunch with a lady friend and a few of his buddies. The sick thing is that he *can* use hundreds as wipes, and there is something very, very wrong with that picture.

The Few

Owners tapped into players' selfish desire for more—a trait etched into our DNA, which may be why humans have secured a hold on this planet, but it may also be the cause of our undoing, as greed is destructive.

Even though major leaguers are *drastically* overpaid, they deserve hefty compensation for their services. Major League Baseball generates tremendous revenue, and those who can compete on the major-league level are rare individuals—special. I've heard people make statements such as:

> *Professional athletes shouldn't make millions, because they're playing ball for God's sake! Doctors save lives and teachers educate our children. Teachers and doctors are the ones who should make the most money!*

I disagree with this analogy. Human beings crave entertainment; it's why we sit in front of the television for hours on end, go to movies, flock to concerts, and attend sporting events. The stories of the Olympic gods would never have survived the millennia if mythology wasn't a form of entertainment for the ancients, and the popularity of the Roman Colosseum is another prime example.

Fans finance the entertainment industry with our hard-earned money because we yearn for it; we simply have to have it. We marvel at the abilities of the select few who are able to do what the average person wants to do, dreams to do, but cannot do. We can't act like Morgan Freeman, fight like Bruce Lee, sing like Andrea Bocelli, or make films like Steven Spielberg, and we sure as hell can't hit a ninety-seven mile per hour baseball that cuts and moves during its .40 second journey from the pitcher's mound to home plate. We probably couldn't even discern if the pitch was a strike or a ball until it was in the catcher's mitt. Another layer of uniqueness regarding pro ballplayers is that they are endowed with major-league confidence. Whether that confidence is in the form of Bernie Williams' quiet cool or Rickey Henderson's in-your-face attitude, it's an essential component of those who can realize a career in the *bigs*. It's like Yogi said, "Ninety percent of this game is half mental." Nobody can sum things up like Lawrence Peter Berra!

Teachers and doctors fill a vital role in society, but there are many more jobs in those fields than there are in pro baseball. The U.S. population is roughly 315 million, and there are an estimated 3.7 million full-time K-12th grade teachers, 900,000 licensed physicians, and 750 major league baseball players (not including expanded rosters). There are merely 3,700 professional athletes between the NFL, NHL, NBA, and MLB combined. So there are 3.7 million teachers, 900,000 physicians, and 750 professional baseball players, and the salaries coincide with those numbers:

- **Teachers: $55,000; Physicians: $350,000; MLB players: $4.25 million.**

Even though physicians do pretty well and most teachers are underpaid (you'd understand if you were a teacher, have children who are teachers, or are married to a teacher), statistics prove that it's near impossible to become a professional baseball player, and, because of their skill-set, major leaguers deserve to make huge money—but the word "huge" is subjective. I contend that pros deserve a lot of money and should be revered, but my reverence does not cloud my common sense. The question everyone should be asking is quite obvious:

Where the hell does it end?

Too many major leaguers become drunk with ego and lose their grip on reality. Most fans live in the real world because our modest existence keeps us grounded in it.

Baseball Cap

I suggest we scrap the current MLB pay scale. I've thought of a system based on production and generous compensation within a finite framework. We are living in a generation where some people want to earn a paycheck just because they get out of bed in the morning, and that provides a destructive model for America's youth. I see it in the classroom, as some students want the A+ even if they don't put in the time or may not have the wherewithal to get the A+.

In my system, MLB players would make a nice paycheck, but they have to earn the monster pay dirt within the parameters of a salary cap. I propose salary tiers. There would be multiple-tier levels within various columns of specific statistics. Each stat category has a monetary value, and when you add up his stats, that's what he gets paid for the year. Teams could entice players to sign with them based on a one-time signing bonus within a capped grid. The bargaining chip is the signing bonus. After a player gets his initial signing bonus, he has to earn a salary based on his performance. Owners would, of course, need to be able to afford the whole team doing well, but that's their challenge. However, the likelihood of everyone doing well is not realistic; players have their highs and lows. Owners should also raise the postseason wage within a capped scale to provide incentive. The teams with the most money could offer their team the highest paycheck for each round of the playoffs or manipulate it any way they wished. For example, an owner could offer his team the lowest pay scale for each playoff round, but if they win the World Series they get a compensation check for the highest amount for every round. This system would both level major-league egos and quell fan resentment when a player gets signed to a fat contract and does not pull his weight. Rookies should take a few years to enter this grid. Prior to that *rooks* would earn a flat salary with a capped signing bonus. This is a *sketch* of a plan that rewards players for their past performance, but they must earn their wage going forward from there. Once the signing bonuses are paid, everyone is equal; the better he plays, the more money he makes. My aim is NOT to create the pay scale for Major League Baseball, my aim to simply say that there are other ways to approach player salaries, because the present system is broken and destroying baseball.

How many times do the Yankees sign a ballplayer who had been playing at a superstar level but then comes to New York and plays far below his past glory? The current system is so flawed that ballplayers are afforded all the perks without any risk. What happens when a player takes a chance, uses cutting-edge-performance-enhancing drugs, raises his numbers, gets a huge contract, and then stops doing steroids because he is now set for life? He doesn't have to do a thing and he's guaranteed the money. What happens when a ballplayer nails his big payday and simply loses his hunger because he's so well fed—physically and emotionally?

Before the end of the reserve clause players *had* to remain hungry if they wanted financial rewards. If you screwed up, you messed with another guy's money, and if the slacker's own financial stakes didn't inspire him, a bunch of angry teammates may have provided appropriate incentive. Remaining hungry is good for the team, for the individual, for baseball.

Jason Giambi and Mark Teixeira are perfect examples of players who were *beasts* before coming to the Yankees. Giambi's batting average with Oakland over a seven-year span was .300—with the Yanks, .260; that's a forty point drop. The last three years Giambi was with Oakland, he averaged .330 and the first three years with the Yankees he averaged .257—a seventy-three point drop! What's absurd is that Giambi got paid more in one year with the Yankees than he did in his eight years with the A's.

What the heck happened to Mark Teixeira? Whether it was injuries, his inability to adjust to the shift, Yankee Stadium pressure, or something else, Mark Teixeira's numbers have fallen dramatically since he came to the Bronx. The following is a tally of Teixeira's batting averages, runs batted in, and hits from 2009 through 2015: **(BA)** .292, .256, .248, .251, .151, . 216, .255 -- **(RBI)** 122, 108, 111, 84, 12, 62, 79 -- **(H)** 178, 154, 146, 113, 8, 95, 100. Teixeira signed an eight-year $180 million contract—an average yearly salary of $22.5 million. Is he okay with the fact that the Yankees guaranteed him almost $200 million and he's not nearly the player he once was? Does he lie awake at night riddled with guilt? I seriously doubt it, because if he felt all that bad he would have asked for salary cut. And even if he gave back half of what he earned, he'd still be set for two lifetimes. Nobody expects anyone to give money back, but I'm illustrating the point that ballplayers are ridiculously overpaid and they have a deal where they reap one hundred percent of the benefits without any accountability if they perform poorly.

Don't even get me started on **Carl Pavano** ($39.95 million to a man who made twenty-six appearances over a four year period); **Kei Igawa** (five years, $46 million, who lasted sixteen games and was booed into the farm system for the rest of his contract); **A.J. Burnett** (five years, $82.5 million); **Alex Rodriguez** (ten years, $275 million); and the list, as you know, is much longer. It angers fans that ticket prices are ludicrous, especially when there is an abundance of sub-par ballplayers making millions. With all this wasted money, owners are *still* making boatloads of cash, players are laughing all the way to the bank, and fans are playing the fool.

The current system has to be ripped apart and reassembled. If owners don't like it, they should sell their teams, and if the players don't like it, they can strike!

In order for the system to be reevaluated, fans have to intercede because players and owners have no reason to change. If a new salary structure were established, the savings must go back to the fans in the form of reasonable ticket prices. Owners of yesteryear didn't have nearly as many income streams as today, so ballpark admission, food, and souvenirs had to play a much more prominent role in financing the team. One way today's owners are making tons of cash is through broadcasting rights; stadium admissions should nearly be a giveaway to fans because we dole out so much for cable. Besides cable, the people of New York helped pay for the new Yankee Stadium through tax dollars—hundreds of millions in tax dollars! The fans pay the Yankees in terms of cable costs, taxes, merchandize, and outrageous ticket prices. If the Yankees were to give more to the fans, they would still have *plenty* of profits leftover. That's capitalism without the ugliness of reprehensible greed. The current model of professional sports is fertilized with most of the seven deadly sins, and whether you are a God-fearing person or not, I'm sure you would agree that lust, gluttony, greed, laziness, wrath, envy, and pride are not traits you're comfortable with, let alone traits you'd like your children exposed to.

PART 3

Goats and Heroes

• • •

"Whoever loves money never has enough."

~ Ecclesiastes 5:10

• • •

Backbone

Time for a pop quiz, and the format is multiple choice. Circle the most correct response: *There are two outs in the bottom of the ninth, the Yankees are losing by one run, and there are men on second and third. Who is the man best suited to win the game?*

A. Bernie Williams
B. Derek Jeter
C. Paul O'Neill
D. Hideki Matsui
E. Scott Brosius
F. Luis Sojo
G. Jorge Posada

The truth is, I'd feel comfortable with any one of those gutsy clutch hitters stepping into the batter's box. I know, I know Luis Sojo… but you have to admit that he was as scrappy as they come, and he got that huge hit against Al Leiter in the 2000 Subway Series. He was also pretty tough against us in the '95 ALDS. Getting back to the quiz. You were correct if you answered C. Paul O'Neill. If you're saying that there cannot be a definitive answer to an opinion question, you're technically right—there is no *correct* answer, but to me Paul O'Neill was the best player of the new era, and the heart and soul of the last Yankees dynasty. He was my favorite Yankee of the 1990s-2000s, as was Donnie Baseball during the Yankees Great Depression, as was Thurman Munson during the resurgence of the late 1970s. I wanted O'Neill up when the game was on the line. Man, I wanted him up any time. Just watching him look at his bat and talk to himself between pitches was signature O'Neill, and he was *always* that intense, *always* into the game—I often wondered what he was saying to himself up there. Steinbrenner got it right when he coined O'Neill a "warrior." He was a man who left it all on the field, and there was nobody tougher on O'Neill than O'Neill. He was a perfectionist, and we loved him for that. Everyone remembers O'Neill's powerful arm, running everything out, playing his hardest every inning of every game, and practicing his swing either in the dugout or over in Babe Ruth's sacred ground in right field.

Remember that ten pitch at bat against Armando Benitez in Game 1 of the 2000 Subway Series where he eventually came around to score? The whole outcome could have changed if the Mets had won the first game at Yankee Stadium. How about the deciding game of the 1997 ALDS when the Yankees were down by one run and Paul came up with two outs and scorched that Jose Mesa fastball off the wall, and O'Neill, with that injured hamstring, stretched a single into a double, eking out every inch and putting his whole being into that slide. They were not getting him—no damned way—and while it may not have been a graceful slide, it was my favorite slide of all time—by any player. Can we ever forget that running catch off Luis Polonia with two outs in the bottom of the ninth to end Game 5 of the 1996 World Series? What happens if Paul doesn't make that catch? He ran it down, hobbling on his ripped-up hamstring, snagged the ball, slapped the padding of the outfield wall, and saved the game. It reminded me of Kerri Strug's heroic performance in the 1996 Olympic Games in Atlanta after she nailed that vault on her destroyed ankle. I think the whole world held a collective breath when Strug charged at full speed down the runway before launching herself off the horse, twisting and flipping through the air with mechanical accuracy before sticking that dramatic landing just ahead of the pain, which had been diluted by the will to win. If you've not seen that, check it out on YouTube. You won't get the full effect because you know the outcome, but it's still thrilling to watch. It's intensely moving when a human being channels the sheer will to succeed—to win when he or she has no business winning, yet despite insurmountable odds, that individual wins the race, hits the basket, makes the catch, nails the landing. That's what Kerri Shrug did in that defining moment in 1996, and that's what Paul O'Neill did time and time again on the baseball field. That's a portion of what O'Neill brought to those historic teams from the middle 1990s through one heart-wrenching night in November 2001; that's what we as Yankees fans became accustomed to, and that's why we love him. How could any of his teammates give anything less than their very best while seeing one of their own giving it his all every moment of every game? In doing that, O'Neill made the whole team better. Just like it's said that Joe DiMaggio made his teams better. It's because that kind of passion cannot be contained—it's contagious and it's the impetus for success.

Do you remember O'Neill's home run off Derek Lowe in the tenth inning when he thought he hit a routine fly ball? Paul threw his bat down in disgust and then watched the ball carry all the way into the seats to tie the game. The man played like there was a war on, and, hence, it was okay with the fans if he slammed some helmets, threw a few bats, or beat a few water coolers into oblivion when he didn't perform to his standard—which was to get a hit *every* time he was at bat—because you can't always turn passion off like a water faucet. I'll take a guy like that playing for the Yankees any day.

The 2001 Yankees verse Diamondbacks World Series was a rough year for America, and it was an odd World Series for the Yankees. When Alfonso Soriano hit the go-ahead home run off Curt Schilling in the 8th inning of Game 7 we thought it was over. However an overworked Mo, holding onto a one-run lead, unraveled before our eyes, became human, blew the save, and lost the game. My heart skipped a beat when Mariano threw that ball into the outfield. There was also bad karma when Jeter got tangled up in David Dellucci's legs and Scott Brosius held the ball at third when he could have made a double play. It was strange to see. It was like a supernatural force had taken over the game and altered what should have been, right before our eyes—like the way angels were altering the events of the living in the film *Angels in the Outfield.*

We lost so much in 2001. No Yankees fan will ever forget the ninth inning of Game 5, as the Yankees were losing 2-0 with the definite possibility of facing a 3-2 deficit heading back to Arizona. O'Neill took his place in right field, Ramiro Mendoza was on the mound pitching to the first batter, Steve Finley, and the chant just happened—

56,000 Yankees fans forgot all about the World Series and began pouring their hearts out with a stirring and thunderous repetition of "Paul O'Neill! Paul O'Neill! Paul O'Neill!" which continued for most of the ninth inning. The Stadium crowd was honoring him the only way they could. I wish I had been there, but as I watched the ninth inning in my living room that night in early November, I felt the hairs standing up on the back of my neck. The Stadium passion spread across the city and to Yankees fans all over the country. The nation saw how much we loved Paul O'Neill, and at that moment it wasn't about winning a pivotal World Series game, it was about paying tribute to a member of our Yankees family—to one of our heroes.

O'Neill was the backbone of the last dynasty because of his gut-wrenching passion on the field, but he's also my favorite player of that era because he wasn't full of himself. While he hadn't embraced the fans as perhaps Nick Swisher had, O'Neill didn't present himself that way either. He seemed uncomfortable in the spotlight; he just wanted to play baseball in New York, and he proved that when he quietly settled his contract with the Yankees prior to its termination. He could have made much more money in a media-fueled bidding war, but he liked playing in the Bronx, he wanted to stay, and he didn't want his life turned into a circus. He is a model for all other players to emulate, not only for his quality of play but for his integrity—his understanding that money is not the most sacred commodity in life. O'Neill didn't pawn his dignity with rounds of debilitating financial debates regarding past injuries, possible injuries, RBI, WAR, OBP, OPS, VORP, a host of other stat acronyms, and what he could get if he bargained with other teams in order to raise the stakes and force the Yankees' hand. Such negotiations lead to resentment, and O'Neill wanted no part of that. What he did want was a contract, which he signed for millions of dollars, to finish his career in pinstripes. He settled for millions, but not *all* the millions he could have squeezed out. The man has honor and, for what it's worth, my utmost respect.

I have a laminated newspaper photograph of Paul O'Neill with his arms around the great Don Zimmer whose head is buried in O'Neill's chest. O'Neill as the parental figure consoling the veteran coach. Paul has a stoic look on his face as he's watching what I suppose to be the jubilant Arizona Diamondbacks celebrating their hard-earned 2001 World Series victory over a team that may turn out to be the last line of the Yankees dynasty. Does anyone think there will ever be another one? It's possible, I guess, but without George at the helm, I have my doubts. However, future dynasties might emerge if the Steinbrenners sell all of their shares to Derek Jeter, on time of course, because even Derek Jeter doesn't have the kind of money to buy the New York Yankees. Jeter running the team would be interesting indeed, because Jeter seems to have hammered out some kind of a sweet deal with the Almighty Himself.

God's Other Son

With Derek Jeter, I've come to expect the unexpected. After Jeter's final game at Yankee Stadium you'd swear he was part of God's inner circle. Jeter had it all—brains, talent, money, women, power, and just the right amount of luck. He was on the right team at the right time, had a manager who loved him, embodied the passion to succeed, and had a gnawing desire to win. Moreover, he scrubbed, honed, and protected a squeaky-clean image, which is a challenge in today's Big Brother society. He was the face of the Yankees and of baseball, and will be a first ballot Hall of Famer who will go down in history as one of the greatest of all time. His accolades legitimize the hype: Rookie of the Year, All-Star MVP and World Series MVP in 2000, seven pennants, five World Series rings, team captain, 3465 hits, .310 lifetime batting average, cool in the clutch, and owner of the famous "flip play" in the 2001 ALDS series and the diving catch against the nemesis Sox in 2004, which left him bloodied and bruised. Derek Jeter may have been every one of those things, but he was never my favorite Yankee.

First, because he didn't embrace the fans as much as his carefully chosen words implied. He delivered his heartfelt lines like a seasoned politician, who had an ever-ready supply of trite phrases built around Yankees fans as being special in some way; yet there was always a distance, coolness, and reserve between him and us. Jeter's relationship with the fans was never, ever, like the fantasy orchestrated in the Gatorade "Made in New York" commercials during his farewell tour. The commercial that's the most Disneyesque is when Jeter, feeling nostalgic, tells his driver to stop the car so he can walk a few blocks to the Stadium. Jeter seizes the moment and immerses himself in the magic of the Bronx atmosphere. He freely signs autographs for awestruck fans, and it's no doubt the fans are shocked, because Jeter isn't known to give autographs freely, let alone for free. We wanted Derek Jeter to be that person, and that's why the masses loved those commercials; it fulfilled their Jeter fantasy—the illusion he propagated. The reality is that Jeter had twenty years to behave that way—to embrace fans—and he never did. It took Gatorade to pay him huge sums of money to create that mirage. Jeter trying to sell a fan-friendly image is about as real as a scene from Sylvester Stallone's *The Expendables*—pure Hollywood. When you think of it though, the commercial was genius; it made Gatorade look great, gave fans the moment they dreamed of, and added a few more zeros to Jeter's already generous bank account. That's a win, win, win, a Derek Jeter motif.

It seems like Jeter always comes out a winner. How about Jeter's 3000th hit caught by twenty-three year old, diehard Yankees fan Christian Lopez? The ball's estimated worth was somewhere in the vicinity of $250,000, and Lopez received, in exchange for giving the prized ball to Jeter, Stadium seats (until the end of the season) and memorabilia. While it's true that the seats and memorabilia had an estimated value of $50,000-$70,000, you can't pay rent or invest in a retirement plan with rented seats at Yankee Stadium. It was Lopez's choice to give the ball to Jeter, but I can't help but feel as though the awestruck fan may have been taken advantage of. When it surfaced that Lopez owed $150,000 in college loans and was employed at a cell phone store, it was clear that Jeter needed to do the right thing and give back to the kind-hearted fan—and something more valuable than signed goods and a few choreographed photos. It was Mitchell Modell, CEO of Modell's Sporting Goods, who stepped up and gave Lopez $25,000 and a genuine Yankees World Series ring. Brandon Steiner matched Modell's $25,000 gift. Miller High Life offered to pay the taxes on the gifts Lopez received from the Yankees.

Mitchell Modell, Brandon Steiner, and Miller High Life were there for Lopez, but where was Jeter? What did he do besides pose for pictures and sign his name on memorabilia? I hope Jeter did the right thing and paid off Lopez's college loans without the popping flashes of the New York media. What's a hundred thousand dollars to a person who is worth over $185 million, especially if the money were given to someone in obvious need? If Jeter cared about the fans as much as he often claimed, he would have paid off the kid's loans—not because Lopez asked for it, but because Lopez didn't ask for it. He gave selflessly, because he was obviously raised with good morals. Lopez didn't give the ball to Jeter for monetary compensation, he offered it to Jeter because it was the right thing to do. Who knows, maybe Jeter did the right thing and helped that young man get a good start in life. I certainly hope so.

As a ballplayer, Jeter is one of the all-time greats who has rightfully earned his place in both Monument Park and Cooperstown. Derek played the game right, never did performance-enhancing drugs or anything to embarrass himself, his family, or the Yankees, but it seems clear that his main priority was building the Derek Jeter financial empire, dollar by dollar.

Of course Jeter was touched by the love Yankees fans poured out to him on his last day at the Stadium, but was he choked up because this was the end of his celebrated career—a goal he had dreamt about and worked towards since he was a small child—or was it because he wouldn't be seeing us anymore?

If it hadn't been for the Yankees giving Jeter his respect in the form of monstrous dollars during his contract negotiations, which were never settled without a battle, Derek would have been just as emotional listening to the fans of Los Angeles, Texas, Houston, Baltimore, or whatever team would have signed him for the cash he demanded if the Yankees didn't buck up to his financial expectations. Would Jeter ever walk into Steinbrenner's office, as O'Neill had, and quietly sign a contract where he would not have gotten top-market value? Not in a million years would he ever do that, and it's a fact because he never did. With Jeter it wasn't about being content with playing shortstop at Yankee Stadium in front of the greatest fans on the planet, it was about respect in the form of colossal contracts. He would lead a clean life, run out every ground ball, and compete for a title, but only if he was paid the most money he and his agent could push for through rounds of heated contract negotiations. That mentality—the mentality of pushing owners to pay shocking, inappropriate salaries in order to pacify greed and ego is the poison that's infected baseball. That's partially to blame for fans getting pushed to the outskirts of Yankee Stadium. Why shouldn't the average family be able to afford seats close to the action once in a while? The American dream for the few has compromised the American pastime for the masses.

We cheered Derek Jeter on to the very last moment of his very last day. That's the reality of our relationship with Jeter, which is far different from the illusion portrayed in the sport drink commercials.

Clutch

I never remember Scott Brosius as someone we feared when he came over from Oakland in 1998, but when he became a Yankee he wreaked havoc on opposing pitchers—especially in the late innings when the game was on the line. Joe Torre had a weapon with Brosius, as he often batted him at the end of the order. Pitchers never had a break against the Yankees in the heart of the dynasty, because even the guy batting ninth could destroy you, and, *man*, did Brosius ever fill that role. Scott Brosius was a favorite of mine for several reasons. He was a clutch player with integrity who didn't take being a Yankee for granted; he was thrilled to play in the Bronx. I remember hearing him say it on several occasions, and it didn't come off as a rote, boilerplate statement. I believed him because his expression was authentic. He was just having fun, loving the New York Yankees, and thrilled to play on the hallowed grounds of Yankee Stadium. And with a salary at around 4.6 million a year, he wasn't paid much in terms of the super-star players of his day, many of whom he outshone.

After the 2001 heartbreaker World Series, Brosius quietly retired from baseball. His reason was that he wanted to spend more time with his family. I'm sure his family was a main factor in his decision, but with the Yankees signing Drew Henson (who?) a third baseman, Brosius saw the writing on the wall even though he batted a solid .287 in 2001 (which would have been roughly the highest batting average on the team as I'm writing this section of the book in 2014) and hit that dramatic two out, two run homer in the bottom of the ninth off Arizona closer Byung-Hyun Kim, tying the game and leaving the door open for Alfonso Soriano to win it in the twelfth. Who could forget his heroics in the 1998 World Series? He was the Series MVP with a .471 batting average and two home runs in Game 3, one off closer Trevor Hoffman, who is second on the all-time saves list just behind Mo. I have a sneaking suspicion Brosius might have stayed if the Yanks had given him some assurance and offered him a respectable deal. If he had to choose between playing baseball in, say, Seattle, a team located fairly close to his home state of Oregon, or retire and be around his family, his obvious choice was to be with his family. If the Yankees really wanted him to stay, I think they could have gotten a year or two more, and he could have made a difference because he was a man who knew how to win.

Brosius made his choice and it certainly wasn't based on money. I have no doubt that he could have gotten a few million playing elsewhere, because he was still a proven clutch hitter, which is a valuable asset to any team, postseason bound or not. Brosius went out playing for the best franchise of all time during the scorching heat of one of the greatest Yankees dynasties. His decision to retire seems to have been based on self-respect and family values—and he's a winner in my book.

Unsung Hero

Another Yankees hero is Andrew Eugene Pettitte, and let's get this straight—Andy never cheated! All the nonsense that's been said about him is nothing but trash! Any sports writer who says that Pettitte cheated should be barred from entering Yankee Stadium. Andy Pettitte used human growth hormone to help him recover from injuries and he did it to help his team. In *The Summer of '49*, author David Halberstam says Joe DiMaggio chain-smoked and drank cups of coffee repeatedly. Caffeine is a drug currently banned by the NCAA, so could we accuse DiMaggio of doping? Caffeine is a stimulant that acts upon the central nervous system speeding messages to and from the brain. It's a drug that helps a person react quicker. Doesn't that give him or her an edge over those who are not doping with caffeine? How much caffeine does it take to produce a positive drug test in the NCAA? Approximately five cups within a two hour period. It sounds like Joe D had at least that many.

Another performance-enhancing compound is creatine, a substance not banned by professional sports or the NCAA; however, there are reports stating that creatine increased the testosterone levels of college football players by a significant amount. An increase in testosterone may give users an edge, right? Am I exaggerating by using caffeine and creatine as examples? Perhaps a little, but my point is that Andy Pettitte played pro baseball for eighteen seasons, and if he were a cheater he would have used anabolic steroids to combat the deluge of roid-powered hulking hitters of his era. Andy Pettitte did not cheat, but what he did do was put up Hall of Fame numbers, and there are voters who will not give him what he earned.

In the article "HGH Mistake Keeps Pettitte from Hall," sportswriter Wallace Matthews talks about how he wouldn't vote for Andy because of Pettitte's admitted use of HGH. The article *fails to mention* that HGH was not a banned substance in the major leagues when Pettitte used it to rehab from injuries. Matthews does, however, mention stat after stat highlighting Pettitte's remarkable career. Lucky for Joltin' "Java Joe" DiMaggio that Wallace Matthews wasn't casting Hall of Fame ballots when he was being considered. I wonder what Matthews' thoughts are on creatine's impact on testosterone levels? Unfortunately Mr. Matthews isn't the only Hall voter who will unfairly block Andy. There may be something, after all, to the rumored anti-Yankees bias in Hall of Fame voting. The Yankees, with twenty-seven championships, are the winningest baseball franchise in history, so it's baffling that Yankees players rank third among Hall of Famers. Not only are the Yankees the best baseball team in history, they are the best by a very wide margin. The next best team, the St Louis Cardinals, have only ten World Championship banners flying at Busch Stadium.

The best teams have the best players, so it's clear that there exists a prejudice against Yankees players among sports writers, and that's the obvious reason why Andy has never won a Cy Young Award. Pettitte had two 21-8 seasons, one in 2003 and the other in 1996, and while Roy Halladay was the clear AL Cy Young Award winner in 2003, Pettitte should have won it in 1996. Pat Hentgen won the American League honors in 1996 with both an excellent 20-10 record and a season that ended in September. Andy's record was 21-8, plus he proved himself through grueling rounds of October baseball. Pettitte played a pivotal role in the Yankees' dismantling of the defending champ Atlanta Braves who may very well have been the better team. Andy came into his own in 1996 and demonstrated his grit and ferocity before the entire baseball world.

Andy's career stats can be held up against some of the greatest pitchers of all time. Pettitte's 3.85 ERA would be the highest in the Hall, but he's only five points above Red Ruffing. Common sense dictates that there will always be someone with the highest ERA, and players are in the Hall because of the breadth of their stats. For example, Pettitte never had a losing season and has totaled 256 career wins, which is more wins than Pedro Martinez, Catfish Hunter, Bob Gibson, Whitey Ford, Don Drysdale, Jack Morris, and other Hall of Famers. Pettitte's winning percentage of .627 bests Cy Young, Tom Seaver, Nolan Ryan, Steve Carlton, Don Sutton, Tom Glavine, Greg Maddux, and John Smoltz—yeah, the last three are from the great Atlanta Braves teams who won division titles from 1991 to 2005, appeared in the World Series three times, and won it all in 1995.

Andy's 60.9 WAR smokes Whitey Ford, Catfish Hunter, Sandy Koufax, Red Ruffing and other legends.

Yet Pettitte's crown jewels are his five World Series rings and his 19-11 postseason record, which happens to make him the **winningest postseason pitcher of all time.** And let's not forget that Houston won their only National League Championship while Pettitte was with them. Coincidence? I don't think so. Isn't winning what the Hall of Fame should recognize? Isn't winning in the postseason and, obviously, the World Series the greatest accomplishment in baseball? The best teams play each other when the stakes are highest. Andy accomplished that better than any pitcher in MLB history, and that's one of the major reasons why he belongs in the Hall.

As a Yankees fan, I like Andy for many of the same reasons I like Paul O'Neill—they are both tenacious gamers who came to play every day, hated to lose, and weren't all about money. The Yankees would have never lost Andy after his stellar 24-9 (includes postseason) 2003 season, if the Yankees had made a respectable attempt at signing him. The Bombers had fifteen days of exclusive negotiations to demonstrate their commitment, but they waited until day fourteen before reaching out to him. It's incomprehensible that Steinbrenner would do that to a proven homegrown Yankee who finished the season with a 24-9 record. It was only after Pettitte gave Houston owner Drayton McLane his word that the Yankees came in with a $39 million dollar offer. Prior to that they made the worst offer of all the teams who coveted him.

Andy Pettitte didn't leave the Yankees because of money; it was obvious that the Yankees were not very interested in his services. The Yankees demonstrated that they really didn't care if Andy pitched elsewhere. This was not only ignorant, it was insulting, especially after all the virtuoso performances by this dauntless veteran. It was thrilling watching Andy battle it out during his legendary postseason showdowns. The drama of his epic duel against the 1996 National League Cy Young winner John Smoltz in Game 4 of the World Series in Atlanta was not only riveting, it was the turning point of the series! When Andy took the mound, deadpan eyes peering out from under the brim of his cap, he revealed his inner predator. Andy was a pit bull—a 6 '5" 225 pound Texas pit bull.

Andy Pettitte may not have had Nolan Ryan's blistering fastball, Ron Guidry's lethal slider, Sandy Koufax's nasty curve, Tom Seaver's svelte ERA, or Cy Young's inhuman 511 wins, but he possessed a fierce competitive spirit, a perfectionist's conviction, the hunger for victory, and the most damned wins in postseason history!

Juiced

While we're on the subject of performance-enhancing drugs, I would be remiss if I didn't mention Roger Clemens who sits squarely atop the steroid scandal—and steroids are a far different animal than human growth hormone. Anti-aging clinics around the country *legally* prescribe human growth hormone every day. In fact insurance covers HGH in some instances, but that will never happen with steroids. Steroids are a monster; Arnold Schwarzenegger and Lou Ferrigno hardly look human in pictures taken of them in the seventies, and body builders of the current era look even more inhuman. Current pro body builder Phil Heath claims he's never used steroids, and perhaps he never has, but did you ever see a human being either in everyday life or at the gym who looks like that? Even if you aren't familiar with Mr. Heath's physique, I'm sure you've seen what I'm talking about. A friend of mine at work, Andy, practically lives in the gym and eats grilled chicken and vegetables with cups of green tea every day, and while Andy is in phenomenal physical shape, he looks nothing at all like Mr. Olympia 2015; Andy looks human, and Phil Heath looks like a shorter version of the Incredible Hulk.

It's hilarious when the steroid-induced-cape-buffalo-looking body builders promote protein drinks, saying that the supplement they are endorsing, which they can hardly lift to their mouths because their biceps are so big, is the key to their muscle growth. There are so many scammers when it comes to money. People trade their dignity for money every single day.

Why do you suppose Clemens, allegedly, used steroids? I say allegedly because he was never found guilty of using them, but the Rocket will never see the Hall of Fame unless he buys a ticket, and that's because there aren't many people who are buying his story. If Clemens had done steroids, the question to explore is why? He didn't need them, as he was a feared pitcher who had killer stats and serious respect. Perhaps he might have used them for a World Series ring. Perhaps he couldn't accept his own mortality. Perhaps because hitters were using them and Clemens was not going to sit back and take it, especially when it seemed dubious that anyone cared. Major League Baseball's *laissez-faire* governing of steroid control made it appear as though they simply looked the other way, because even fans knew what was going on.

I remember talking about it, as home runs were getting jacked out of the park like it was some kind of prank during the Mark McGwire/ Sammy Sosa home run derby of 1998. Baseball, which had been dipping in popularity, suddenly became more exciting; there was a buzz around baseball that couldn't have hurt cash flow. Raging, reconstructed, steroid titans were appearing all over the majors. Barry Bonds who weighed 185 in 1986 wound up resembling a California Redwood by 2001 when he tipped the scales at 228. Just Google before and after photos of Mark McGwire, Sammy Sosa, Jason Giambi, Barry Bonds, Jose Canseco, Alex Rodriguez, and David Ortiz. All of these players either admitted to steroid use or appeared on a list that was published by *The New York Times* in 2009. The report lists David Ortiz as one of a hundred players who tested positive for PEDs in 2003. Ortiz denies that he ever used PEDs and that the positive result may have been triggered by supplements he was taking. It's especially amusing because when he was asked by reporters which supplements may have caused the false positive, Ortiz said he didn't know. How original.

People have been skeptical about Ortiz for years and for good reason. Ortiz averaged around 15 home runs a year when he was with the Twins; he belted 20 *dingers* in 2002 during his final year in Minnesota. There are three glaring points that are significant about 2003: Big Papi signs with the Red Sox, his power numbers surge (31 home runs), and he tests positive for PEDs. From that point on, Big Papi's home run numbers go from good to epic: **2003** - 31; **2004** - 41; **2005** - 47; **2006** - 54. That's not just amazing, it's pretty damned suspicious. However, when David Ortiz dropped sixty-eight points off his batting average between 2007 and 2008, people were saying his career was over. When his average dropped even further to .238 in 2009—a nearly one hundred-point drop over a two year period, people assumed that retirement was imminent. David Ortiz got the name Big Papi because... he's pretty big, and carrying extra weight around eventually takes a toll on the body, right? One might assume, but Ortiz amazingly began improving with age. His batting average went from .238 in 2009 to .309 in 213, a year that included 30 home runs, and what might be just as amazing is that the thirty-seven-year-old giant, who is not particularly light of foot, had 2 triples!

During the 2013 World Series, the same year fourteen players were suspended for being named in the Biogenesis steroid debacle, World Series MVP Big Papi batted .688, with 2 home runs, 6 RBI, and he reached base 19 out of 25 times. The question is, if David Ortiz used steroids in 2013 why didn't he get caught? I have no idea, but it's not like other people didn't get away with it. Admitted steroid user Alex Rodriguez was tested numerous times while he was using PEDs, but he turned up clean. A-Rod appeared at the center of the steroid scandal after a former disgruntled Biogenesis of America employee blew the whistle and uncovered the truth about Anthony Bosch's clinic.

Most people agree that steroids are wrong and are a form of cheating, but the line gets fuzzy in many other instances. For example, there is a split decision around the supposed *dirty* slide by Chase Utley in the 2015 NLDS which resulted in Ruben Tejada's broken leg. There were kids in my class arguing about it the day after it happened. Was the slide cheating or gamesmanship? Who determines what cheating is? Of course there are rules governing the game, but rules are open for interpretation. Is sign stealing really cheating? How about ball doctoring? There are reports of numerous pitchers—some Hall of Famers, who were either accused of or openly admitted to cutting or scarring the ball or using substances such as Vaseline, mud, baby oil, turpentine, and resin in order to make the ball do what it cannot do unless it is manipulated. How about bat caulking, Superball loaded bats, or field doctoring? Cheating or gamesmanship? Some teams have soaked the field with water for either their sinkerball pitchers or to make the area around base paths soft for opposing teams with speed. Some teams raised baselines to keep bunts fair—only if their team had a good bunter, of course. It's said that one year the Chicago White Sox had three great pitchers and absolutely no offense, so they kept baseballs in a room with a humidifier, and after twelve days they became a quarter to a half ounce heavier. Sounds a lot like Deflategate. Did the New England Patriots cheat? The NFL believes they did, and if the Patriots did, the Chicago White Sox look pretty darn guilty. Even the great Babe Ruth injected himself with extract from sheep testicles. Luckily it made him sick and he didn't try it again or his reputation might be tainted. It's said, however, that while the Babe was interested in knocking balls out of the park, he was very intrigued by what the sheep testicle extract might add to his bedroom stamina. According to reports, the Bambino was quite the ladies' man. Ping Bodie, a roommate of Ruth, claimed that the Babe went through every girl in a Philadelphia brothel on two consecutive nights. And while that may seem like a tall tale, there are stories upon stories about Ruth's superhuman libido, which leads me to believe that if there were a hall of fame for lovers, a plaque of George Herman Ruth would stand smack between Genghis Khan and Wilt Chamberlain.

Gamesmanship? Cheating? Is there a difference? Through all of this, one thing is clear: Roger "Rocket Man" Clemens and all of the players of the steroid era are blacklisted and will never, in the eyes of many, be anything other than players who cheated. I guess it was their fate, since Major League Baseball and most everyone else concerned seemed to look the other way at first.

Using anabolic steroids is cheating because steroids are illegal drugs that are banned from all major sports. The fines and suspensions for steroids are still too lenient. Moving forward, any player found guilty of doping should be suspended for a minimum of three seasons without pay, be given a fine that's based on a percentage of his current contract, and have all statistics erased for the year of the offense. A strict policy of that depth would deter players from using steroids.

Clemens is out of hot water with the law, but he has to live the rest of his life with a dark cloud hanging over his integrity and stats. When most people think of Roger Clemens they won't envision one of the greatest pitchers of all time, they will think of his steroid scandal.

*Hearts and Hands

The polar opposite of guys like Andy Pettitte, Scott Brosius, and Paul O'Neill is David *Turncoat* Cone. I can't believe he's allowed to step foot into Yankee Stadium—let alone have a job there. Couldn't he find something with the Boston Red Sox? Perhaps the Sox wanted him but the Yankees offered him more money. Not sure and really don't care, because there's one thing David Cone revealed about himself: it's all about money. Many of my Yankee brothers and sisters might question my sentiments for Cone, who happens to be *one* of only *three* Yankees who ever pitched a perfect game, but I've never forgiven him for jumping ship in 2001.

Cone had been one of my favorite Yankees because he was the right man at the right time in 1995, our hired gun whose presence and skill solidified the Yankees' position as American League contenders. He was a real pitcher—crafty as hell. He had the guile of Odysseus on that hill during many epic battles at Yankee Stadium, and he was very likable—his commercials, awesome! I liked the one where he's in a night club with Luis Sojo and the dance floor is crowded with people doing the "El Duque" dance, and Luis Sojo looks at David and says, "Hey Coney, why don't you have a dance?" The commercial ends with a mortified Cone getting busted in the bathroom doing a silly dance move. An even better Cone commercial was the one that featured the "ANSKY" guys (five large shirtless men sitting in the back of a cab and the cabbie asks them what the hell ANSKY means) who help Cone recover from his aneurism surgery, by giving him a "hand" with everything. Cone's face after he exits the bathroom stall is priceless. Not only could Cone pitch, but he proved he had some acting chops. That commercial was even better than the Luis Tiant Yankee Franks spot of the 1970s.

Cone had me fooled as he professed his love for the Yankees with that sincere, contemplative, puppy-dog countenance, saying that he wanted to end his career in pinstripes. I was shocked when his true nature emerged after his contract ended in 2000. Cone had no problem cashing his $12 million paycheck while going 4-14 with a 6.91 ERA—no problem at all! After his humbling exhibition in 2000, he had the *gall* to turn down a $500,000 one-year contract from the Yankees, yet accepted a $1,000,000 contract with the Yankees' greatest rival. He chose to pitch against us—the fans, his teammates, his manager—on a regular basis, and to do his part to beat us, and he *did* try to beat us. He committed the greatest of Yankee sins. This isn't the same as a player who is released or traded to a rival club. *Benedict Arnold* Cone chose to play against his former team because Boston offered him $500,000 more than the Yankees had. The Yankees paid Cone nearly $40 million over his five plus years with them, and he totaled just under $67 million in his career, yet he chose to play against us for $500,000. That's a disgrace! He didn't feel an obligation to accept what the Yankees offered him after his abysmal, Class-A pitching performance of 2000?

I would have been angry if he had chosen to leave the Yankees for *any* team after all the baloney he shoveled to the media about his love for the team, tradition, and fans, but not as furious as I was when he decided to pitch for Beantown.

Again, how much money does a person need? The greed of these athletes is loathsome—repulsive! Where is their honor? Cone should have hung his head in shame, instead he told Boston's general manager at the time, Dan Duquette, that he had every intention of beating the Yankees. Boston wound up paying Cone a total of $1 million, and, according to reports, the deal had incentives that could have earned him between $4 to $5 million—but it was not guaranteed and there was a catch. Boston could have let Cone go during spring training and pay him a termination fee of around $16,000. And while Cone didn't come close to the 4-5 million dollar incentive package Boston waved in front of him, he had a winning season (9-7), and he pitched against the Yankees to the best of his ability. Remember Mike Mussina's near perfect game in 2001? After retiring twenty-six successive Red Sox batters, Earl Everett singled on a 1-2 count to spoil Mussina's brush with history. Do you remember who was pitching his heart out against the Yankees that game? Boston Red Sox pitcher David Cone was the man on the hill, and he used every trick he had—every ounce of his will to beat the Yankees. He shut out his former team right into the ninth inning before allowing an unearned run.

Let me illustrate the difference between David Cone and a person with integrity. The Boston Red Sox offered Andy Pettitte a $52 million contract in 2003, which was approximately $22 million more than the Yankees originally offered and $13 million more than the Yankees finally offered, and Pettitte turned them down flat because he couldn't pitch for the Yankees' rival. David Cone's words are far from his actions, as he's proved that it's not about fans, or team, or tradition, or integrity—it's about money. I wasn't surprised when I read that David Cone was out as commentator for the YES Network at one point because of some kind of argument, but David *Silicone* Cone was eventually back in the YES Network booth and still a "valued" member of the Yankees family, to the pleasure of many Yankees fans—obviously not this one.

**"Hearts and Hands" (David Cone's chapter title) is a short story by O. Henry where conning is the principal topic. One character is arrested for counterfeiting, another character is conned into believing a spontaneous tale, and the reader is conned until the very last line of the story.*

Cash Cash

Another Yankee who should be booed out of Yankee Stadium is Carsten Charles "CC" Sabathia. He is the personification of what is wrong with both baseball and society. In 2009 CC signed a seven-year $161 million contract with the Yankees that made him the highest paid starting pitcher in history, and then after winning his only World Series in 2009, the big man seized an opportunity to suck more money out of the Steinbrenner udder in 2011 after exercising his opt-out clause. CC's historic contract had four years remaining at $23 million per year, which totaled $92 million. The new contract guaranteed CC 122 million over five years, which totaled $30 million more than the first contract. People like CC are why fans have to pay a fortune for anything embellished with an interlocking NY.

Sabathia had everything: fame, money, a World Series ring, and respect. He still has everything with the exception of respect. He traded that away to pile more millions onto the huge pile of millions he had already accumulated—a stash he could live on for ten lifetimes. Yes, he is that arrogant and that narcissistic.

Who do you think you are, CC? Do you honestly think that any human being is worth that kind of money? You throw a damned baseball! And while you were able to throw it like an ace for a few years, you still throw a damned baseball! Why opt out of a multimillion dollar historic contract for more millions? Why?

From early in the 2011 season, CC refused to speak about the impending opt-out clause. Why do you suppose he was mum? Isn't it obvious that not showing his hand was a strategic move, a passive aggressive tactic—a seed of doubt planted in the minds of financially fit baseball teams everywhere? He had every intention of opting out since the day he signed the original contract. If he had a good year in 2010, the Yankees would sweeten an already diabetes-inducing pie. Rather than face the free-agent market, CC agreed to a new deal that added $30 million and one season to his existing contract.

CC did his little song and dance routine where he said his wife and kids loved New York and he loved pitching for Yankees fans "and everything," and so it was an easy decision to stay here. I distinctly remember him say "and everything." CC also said that it *wasn't* about money, it was about *time*; he wanted more *time*. Does he think we are that stupid? Did Sabathia forget how to do basic math? Hey CC, your new contract pays you $30 million more than your original deal. Perhaps it's because you make so much money that a mere $30 million isn't anything to you. That must be it, because you said that it was *time* and *not* money. Nice try CC… If it was all about being a Yankee then why didn't you go to the Yankees brass and say something like:

> *I love pitching for Yankees fans and everything. You've treated me like a king by placing me at the center of a team that was World Series bound, paid me more money than any starting pitcher had ever made in the history of the game, so I'll sign a new contract with more time and no opt-out clause or anything like that for the same $23 million per year I agreed to in 2009.*

CC's contract extension went down to the wire too, and the two sides were reported as working hard to hammer out an acceptable deal for the big man and his agent, Brian Peters. The Yankees made CC an offer and he came back with a counteroffer. Doesn't a counteroffer indicate that the deal needed to be better? We can assume that he didn't counteroffer fewer dollars, saying something like:

> *No guys, I just wanted more time and everything, not more money. C'mon what are you doing? Put that checkbook away and let's get me some more time!*

After the new contract was sealed CC Tweeted that he'd be trying hard for number twenty-eight. Here's my interpretation of CC's Tweet:

> *Hey fans, my agent just made me a whole lot richer and everything by getting me a new deal on my already absurdly offensive contract. Dudes, I got another $30 million! But hey, keep working hard and feed the*

Yankees money machine so people like me can take advantage of the whole insane system... LOL... JK... not really... LOL. Oh, and BTW, I'll be fighting for number twenty-eight next year, but who cares if we win, lose, or I get hurt, because... I get paid anyway! You guys are great—the best fans in baseball!

In 2011, the infamous opt-out year, CC went 19-8, but what the stat line doesn't show is that he was 0-1 in his final three starts of the season, and he didn't win a game in the 2011 ALDS against the Tigers. Sabathia did, however, give up the winning run in a Game 5 relief appearance, which cost his team the playoffs. Do you remember when the great Randy Johnson pitched in relief against the Yankees in Game 7 of the 2001 World Series on virtually no rest and shut them down? That's what aces do, and it's what CC probably could have done when he was an ace, but he no longer had the tools. He was out of gas, his best days behind him, and the writing was on the wall. He must have known that his best days were behind him and he wanted one last sack of cash. Sabathia's record since he's with the Yankees paints a clear picture of his rapid decline: **2009**: 19-8, 2010: 21-7, **2011**: 19-8 (signs new contract at the end of 2011), **2012**: 15-6, **2013**: 14-13, **2014**: 3-4, **2015**: 6-10.

They should have let Cash Cash go bye bye and used his Brinks-truck salary to invest in other prospects. I wouldn't be surprised if the Yankees release him before his contract expires.

*Lotus Eater

Time for another pop quiz. This shouldn't even count because it's too easy, but I have a tendency to throw in a few easy quizzes to balance out the harder ones. Circle the most correct response:

It's the postseason and there are two outs in the bottom of the ninth, the Yankees are losing by one run, and there are men on second and third. Who is the man you do NOT want stepping up to the plate?

A. Bernie Williams
B. Derek Jeter
C. Paul O'Neill
D. Hideki Matsui
E. Scott Brosius
F. Robinson Cano
G. Jorge Posada

The answer is Robinson Cano, and if you got it wrong you missed the most important word in the question: "postseason." Robbie consistently hits the hell out of the ball from opening day until the end of September, but he's a different player in the postseason, and that's one of the reasons why I wasn't too broken up when he decided skip town for Seattle. If you're on the Yankees, I want you to be able to perform in the requisite second season. Players like Robinson Cano shine in the regular season, but shoot the team in the foot when the pinstripes get heaviest. Real talent lies in the October heroes. Compare Cano's postseason performance with a few of his contemporaries, by way of regular season batting average (REG), postseason batting average (POST) and difference between them (+/-). The numbers speak for themselves:

> **Hideki Matsui** - REG .282, POST .312, (+30); **Derek Jeter** - REG .310, POST .308, (-2); **Paul O'Neill** - REG .288, POST .284, (-4); **Scott Brosius** - REG .257, POST .245, (-12); **Robinson Cano** - REG .310, POST .222, (-88).

While Cano was with the Yankees, his postseason batting average was eighty-eight points lower than his regular season batting average, and it's not that he only played in a few October games. Cano was involved in eleven postseason series over an eight-year period while playing in fifty-one postseason games. This isn't a slump; it's who he is as a player. In 2012, his last postseason as a Yankee, Cano batted .073 and in the Yankees

2009 World Series run, Cano's batting average was a paltry .188. When people make statements such as "Robinson Cano was the best player on the Yankees," they are judging him based on the regular season. That caliber of player may be okay for a team like the Seattle Mariners, but not for the winners of forty AL pennants and twenty-seven World Series. By that account Cano is a perfect fit for the Mariners—no pressure, no real October expectations.

Another reason why I'm not teary-eyed over his ungraceful departure is because he is another living example of how greed distorts one's psyche. Cano got booed at Yankee Stadium, and rightly so, during his first series back as a member of the Mariners. I say "rightly so" because Cano had the audacity to say that the Yankees slighted him when it came to their contract offer. The Yankees offered him $25 million a year for seven years. Captain Derek Jeter, who fought the Yankees hard for his money, never made more than $22 million in a single season, and Robinson Cano had the nerve to say the Yankees showed him no respect. Does he know what the *hell* he's talking about? What astounds me are those, especially sports writers/commentators, who said it was classless for Yankees fans to boo Cano. A colleague of mine said that the Mariners' offer was Cano's only move. Only move? There was another move—accept the $175 million dollars the Yankees offered him. Reasoning like this is a further example of how twisted our society has become; money has eviscerated our virtues—money has become everything. How much can you buy? What luxuries do you want that cost more than what can be bought on $175 million?

I remember another disagreement I had with a sports fan who said that Mike Trout was "stupid" for signing a six-year $144.5 million deal with the Los Angeles Angels because he could have gotten way more if he had become a free agent. Millions upon millions aren't enough for one person when that person could have more and more millions, right? It's sick! Johnny Damon was out of touch as well, regarding his need of financial rewards to stroke his colossal ego; however, Damon and Cano are not cut from the same cloth. Damon hustled, he had a burning desire to win, and he thrived in the postseason; he was a gamer. You *want* Damon on your team in the postseason. It's unfortunate that he turned down the Yankees two-year $14 million contract after the 2009 season. That was the beginning of the end for Damon as he went from the Tigers, where his power numbers tanked because Comerica Park is huge, to the Rays, and to the Indians where he was released mid-season. I think he would have done much better if he had stayed with the Yankees and their friendly right-field porch.

Parents should make their children read Alexander Pushkin's "The Tale of the Fisherman and the Fish," Aesop's "The Goose That Laid the Golden Egg," and the Greek myth about King Midas, yearly; this literature reminds and warns us of the consequences of avarice.

When a ballplayer is compensated with the kind of money Cano got from Seattle, the team's intention, it would seem, is to build around that player. Seattle made a huge mistake if they intend to build a team around Cano. They invested heavily in a position player who both drops eighty-eight points off his regular season batting average in the postseason and doesn't have a burning desire to win. Cano is the antithesis of players like Derek Jeter, Pete Rose, Joe DiMaggio, and Dustin Pedroia. Joe DiMaggio was once asked why he hustled on a play that meant nothing in a game that had little bearing on the Yankees' fate that year, and Joe said he hustled like that because there may be a kid who might be seeing him for the first time and he owed that kid his best. That's class; that's self-respect; that's dignity! It's obvious that Cano doesn't have that kind of respect for the game, himself, or the fans. It would have been interesting to see Robinson Cano and Jonathan Papelbon on the same team. We saw how that turned out for Bryce Harper in 2015, as Harper's "lack of hustle" sparked Papelbon to ream him out and then choke him against a dugout wall before they were separated by a swarm of teammates.

There are numerous reports detailing how Yankees players and staff talked with Cano about his lack of hustle. He's been endowed with incredible talent, but there are athletes born with less natural ability who are more valuable to both the team and the game of baseball. Cano is durable, he likes to play, but he simply doesn't have the passion of veritable Yankees heroes. Cano seemed to me as a boy having fun playing a game. He is too content, lackadaisical—not the type of player who could carry a team.

Some sports writers and people I've encountered claim that Cano wasn't offered enough by the Yankees, but it's clear to me that the Yankees offered Cano far more than he's worth. Committing to that kind of money would have hurt the team in the long run. Cano was a homegrown Yankee who let his hubris and greed get in the way of a glorious lifelong career in pinstripes playing second base for the best team and the best fans in world. That's some of what the Yankees offered him along with the $175 million, and the contract they offered him was not disrespectful; however, what the Yankees did to the next two players truly is.

**Lotus Eaters (Robinson Cano's chapter title) are lethargic characters from Homer's The Odyssey.*

Disrespect For A Champion

In 2006, my son Michael and I traveled to Camden Yards to watch the Yankees play the Baltimore Orioles. We got to the park early in hopes of meeting the Yankees as they walked in, but by the time we found the right entrance, we were told that we just missed Joe Torre, and I wanted to talk to him because he bought a house in my neighborhood in Mahopac, New York. I moved there in 1991, and I wanted to tell him about this pizzeria that bought their Italian ices from De Lillo's Pastry Shop on East 187th Street in the Bronx's Little Italy. If you've never had Italian cream ices from Little Italy, you don't know what you're missing. It's a cross between ice and gelato. Anyway, I was bummed that I didn't get to meet my *paisan.* I never got to meet Joe Torre, but, coincidentally, I met the other Joe (Girardi) in Mahopac at an autograph signing in the late 1990s. It was memorable because it was the zenith of the Yankee dynasty and I'm not sure which bench-clearing brawl it was, but my father, my son, and I met Girardi the following morning. Joe looked like he was hurting with fatigue and probably wished he hadn't agreed to this public-relations event. When it was my turn, I said something like "Great game last night." Joe didn't go there, so I let it lie.

Speaking of brawls, the most famous Yankees skirmish of that era erupted when Armando Benitez drilled Tino Martinez in the back. I'll never forget the Yankees bullpen, led by Graeme Lloyd and Jeff Nelson, bolting down the field toward the pitcher's mound. Graeme Lloyd threw the first punch and Jeff Nelson almost took Benitez' head off with a roundhouse right. Benitez ducked and then started throwing, and mostly missing, weird open-handed punch/slaps. Mike Stanton went summersaulting after he got pushed and was then grabbed by Orioles' catcher, Chris Hoiles, who happened to be in full gear.

It astounds me when catchers' rumble in full gear. Remember when Jason Varitek pulled that crap after A-Rod was intentionally hit by Bronson Arroyo, because hitting batters was part of Boston's game plan back then? The thing is, Varitek initiates the physical fight, yet leaves all of his gear on—metal bars across his face and all. I lost some respect for Varitek that day, because that was a *cowardly* thing to do. If you're going to be a tough guy, be a tough guy. Some ballplayers don't get involved in field brawls, and that's fine, but if you're a catcher and you start fighting, take off your face mask.

Back to the Baltimore brawl... Do you remember that funny moment when the mob of players cleared and Brosius found himself one-on-one with an angry 6' 4" Armando Benitez? Brosius knew better than to attack, and while Benitez was moving toward Brosius, Darryl Strawberry hammered Benitez with a shot that drove Armando into the dugout. People called it a sucker punch, and, yeah, it was, but Benitez deserved that and more for hitting Tino.

Those Yankees teams stuck together back then. Darryl Strawberry seemed like a big brother to the young players. I loved Darryl. Do you remember when he hit that homer off Bret Saberhagen in the 1999 ALCS when the Boston crowd was chanting "Just say no, Just say no" because of Darryl's addiction issues? After Strawberry crushed it off the netting of the Pesky Pole, there was audio of hitting coach Chris Chambliss saying,

"Just say yes, baby, just say yes!" Chambliss is another one of favorite Yankees. Who could forget Chambliss rounding the bases while fighting off fans as he sent the Yankees to the '76 World Series? I've digressed from the story at hand, but it's so easy to get carried away when talking Yankees. Back to Camden Yards in 2006.

So my son and I were waiting for the Yankees to enter Camden Yards with a handful of other Yankees fans who hoped to meet some players. We met Andy Phillips who signed autographs and hung around with us for a bit, and then we got a chance to exchange jibes with Kevin Millar who was then playing for the fourth place Baltimore Orioles. Someone yelled, "You used to be cowboy up and now you're cowboy down," and he responded with "Boston Nation" to which people responded with "Boston sucks," and other such phrases. It didn't get ugly—just Yankees fans letting Millar know that he was still part of the rivalry; he looked like he enjoyed the exchange just as much as we did.

Cory Lidle stopped to talk with us, and he was in great spirits. It was the day after his Yankees debut where he gave up one run over six innings, and it looked like the Yankees just landed a legitimate star. He spoke with us like we were peers—not fans; we were just a few guys talking baseball. I never had an actual conversation with a Yankee before that day. It's kind of cool talking to a pro baseball player, and I don't care how old you are. I clearly remember a day back in the late '60s or early '70s when I saw Mel Stottlemyre as he was warming up. I yelled something down to him like "Hi Mel." He looked up with a smile and said, "Hi." That was it—but he looked like he was glad I said hello to him, and I was the happiest kid in the park that day! Yesterday they honored Mel at Old-Timers' Day, and it was good to see him back at the Stadium again. He said he wasn't sure if he'd see another Old-Timers' Day, which was sad to hear, but I sure hope he does. Mel's still only seventy-four, but even at seventy-four he lived twice as long as Cory Lidle. I was saddened by Lidle's death, firstly because anyone dying at the age of thirty-four is heartbreaking, but also because of those fifteen minutes he spent talking with us outside Camden Yards a few months prior to his passing. He seemed like he was a good guy—the complete opposite of Melky Cabrera. Melky strutted about five feet away from us that day without acknowledging our presence. We called to him, but he didn't even look our way. I thought, "What an arrogant little *shit*!" That was Melky's second year in the *bigs* and he had already developed a pretentious air.

When my son and I entered Camden Yards we saw the Yankees in their road grays, which was strange, having never seen them "in person" without the pinstripes, and standing midfield having conversation with a few players was Bernie Williams—the hero of this passage. My son shouted Bernie's name in a thundering voice. Bernie seemed to have stopped talking mid-sentence, and he turned around in the direction of the sound. My son and I gave him roundhouse waves and he waved back. I had always believed that Bernie was a humble guy, but I was convinced of it that day.

I still can't get over how disgracefully the Yankees treated Bernie in 2007. Since this is a book built upon the theme of greed, I can't discuss Bernie and not mention that he and his agent Scott Boras went to the mats with the Yankees after the '98 season and Bernie was compensated handsomely. However, Bernie went to Steinbrenner, when a $91.5 million deal with Boston seemed imminent, and told George how much he wanted to stay. The Yankees came back with a seven-year offer, and that kept Bernie in pinstripes for the rest of his career. Did Bernie try for as much money as he could get? Yes, but he wasn't only about money; he took $4.5 million less than what Boston offered him, and that says something about Bernie's character. Bernie Williams was a lifelong Yankee who played hard, ran everything out, lived a clean life, and produced in both the regular season and postseason. Finally, he is a five-time All-Star, a four-time Gold Glove winner, and, as of 2015, is ranked within the top ten Yankees in nearly every significant category:

base on balls, intentional base on balls, singles, doubles, home runs, hits, runs batted in, sacrifice flies, runs scored, total bases, games played, and position player WAR.

Bernie also holds a stellar postseason ranking in various categories among *all* players:

> **Base on balls, singles, doubles, home runs, hits, runs batted in, runs scored, total bases, and games played.**

One reason why Bernie's numbers are among the best in postseason history is because he had been there so often; however, the fact that his name appears atop those charts and categories, proves that he was able to excel when it counted the most. Players like Bernie Williams, Paul O'Neill, Tino Martinez, Jorge Posada, Derek Jeter, Hideki Matsui, Scott Brosius, or Darryl Strawberry are the ones who make teams win championships. When Bernie's contract ended after the 2005 season, the Yankees declined the remaining year's option, paid Williams a $3.5 million buy-out, and re-signed him for $1.5 million, a bargain it turns out considering Williams' respectable .281 batting average in 2006. The slap in the face came in 2007, when the Yankees did not offer Bernie a contract, but invited him to spring training on a non-roster basis. After all the World Series rings, all the records, all the stats, all the hustle, all the heart, after sixteen years of quality service, the Bombers insulted one of the all-time Yankee greats with non-roster invitee status after he had a good season. Bernie had to fight for a spot if he wanted to make the team to which he gave so much.

I was sad when Bernie didn't report to spring training that year, but Bernie went out on his terms. According to Scott Boras, other teams offered Williams guaranteed contracts in 2007, but Bernie proved what he said to George Steinbrenner in 1998; he wanted to finish his career as a Yankee. The Yankees lost out and so did we, because they had a man who would have been a presence in the clubhouse—someone to show the kids how it's done. He could have been like a Chili Davis, Cecil Fielder, Tim Raines—a seasoned veteran who knew how to win. The Yankees finally did the right thing by Bernie in 2015 by retiring his No. 51 and giving him a plaque beyond the center-field wall—but this political peace offering came far too late.

Bernie, if you're reading this, I just want to say "thank you" for all you did for the Yankees and for the fans. Thank you for the memories, the hustle, the determination, the championships, and the class. You have *class*, and the never-ending respect of millions of Yankees fans.

Here is the Joe Girardi autograph I got when he was signing in Mahopac, New York, the day after the big Yankees brawl.

When the Yankees were at the apex of their dynasty, my son called me and shouted that he got Paul O'Neill's autograph. It was Michael's eleventh or twelfth birthday, and he and some friends were at the Toys "R" Us in the White Plains Pavilion Mall. One of Michael's friends spotted Paul O'Neill with two young boys, presumably O'Neill's sons. My son and his companions raced out of the store to buy baseballs at the Sports Authority next door. They rushed back to Toys "R" Us and found O'Neill with a PlayStation in hand. Paul was good enough to sign their baseballs and he also took a picture with them, but the picture alerted other shoppers to the iconic right fielder's presence. O'Neill, seeing a crowd come his way, dropped the PlayStation and hightailed it with his kids out the back exit. I asked Michael what he said to O'Neill. Michael said he didn't say anything. I said "You had to say something." It turns out that Michael ran up to O'Neill, and, without saying a word, handed him a baseball and a pen. Michael said he was too nervous to say anything. I said, "You could have asked him if he'd please sign your baseball." I can't blame my son though, I guess most kids would be awestruck if they ran into one of their heroes at a neighborhood mall. It's a little late Paul, but thanks for being a gentleman. Even though my son was only a kid at the time, that baseball is a treasured possession of the now twenty-eight year old man.

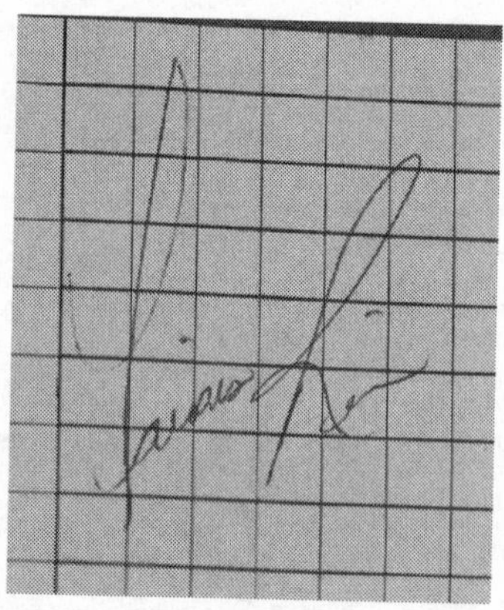

The year was 1995 and I took my kids to Yankee Stadium. We got there extra early so we could watch batting practice. While the Yankees were on the field we made our way over to the section between first base and right field, as fans were gathering there. Two rookies appeared and walked up to the ocean of waving books, pens, baseballs, shirts and other paraphernalia; I happened to get both of their signatures. My kids asked me who they were, but I had no idea. As luck would have it, those two rookies, who were greener than the Stadium lawn, were Andy Pettitte and Mariano Rivera. I'm not sure why, but I remember that day very clearly. Mariano seemed slightly uneasy amid the swarm of energetic Yankees fans, but Andy was sweating and nervous. Pettitte blew out his breath a few times, as one might do before tackling a major task; he was overwhelmed for sure. Who would have known that two of the greatest pitchers of the era would have walked out and signed autographs together? Maybe since it was the year after the strike, the Yankees sent rookies out for some positive PR, although it may have also been some kind of hazing ritual.

Dis-Honored

One of the most exciting players to watch after the last Yankees dynasty was No. 55, Hideki Matsui. He arrived in 2003, in an era where the Yankees were just a player or two short of a championship team, and Hideki played most of his Yankees tenure during the A-Rod years. Many of us thought A-Rod might have been the one we needed—the *key* to the next dynasty. After all, he was arguably the best player at the time—a Gold Glove infielder with legitimate power and an MVP Award. However, there are several publications that featured articles illustrating the repugnant details of how atrociously Jeter treated A-Rod when Alex arrived in 2004. After hearing the reports, I surmised that Jeter's actions may have cost the Yankees World Championships—perhaps another World Series run.

It was A-Rod who drew first blood in the feud when he foolishly attacked his once "best friend" during a radio interview in 2000. A-Rod said that he made more money than Jeter because he (A-Rod) had the power numbers. Rodriguez also insinuated that he was better than Jeter defensively. He made other demeaning comments a few months later, saying Jeter never had to carry a team, and that teams don't sweat number-two hitters. This went over about as well as Reggie Jackson's comments about "the straw that stirs the drink." It's reported that it didn't take long for A-Rod to figure out that he'd made a huge mistake, but it was too late. The word is that once you screwed with Jeter you were "dead" to him. Alex begged for forgiveness, but Jeter was ice cold.

A-Rod was playing for Texas when the interviews were released in 2000 and 2001, but a few years later, in 2004, A-Rod and Jeter were sharing some of the same real estate on the left side of the infield at Yankee Stadium, and the atmosphere was tense. It is said that Yankees officials, including Brian Cashman, tried convincing Jeter to cut the nonsense, and even Don Mattingly tried getting through to the Captain by saying that *he* had issues with Wade Boggs when Boggs came over from Boston in '93. Mattingly had to let it go because he and Boggs were teammates. It seems that Alex found himself squarely wedged between a rock and a hard place because he was in Jeter's house and Derek was a four-time World

Champion and New York Yankees legend. Whether it was the pressure-cooker clubhouse atmosphere or just good old-fashioned guilt, A-Rod was obsessed with trying to make amends, and Jeter was making him eat crow. It all came to a head when Jeter lost his cool in front of fifty thousand fans at Yankee Stadium and a few hundred thousand more on TV. The infamous incident occurred when a pop-up hung between short and third and both players went for it. Jeter bumped into A-Rod and the ball popped out of A-Rod's glove. Jeter stared at A-Rod with disgust and then walked away without picking up the ball even though it was closer to him.

Blinded by unfettered hubris, the elephantine egos of both Derek Jeter and Alex Rodriguez collided head on, and the result was not unlike the massive comet that struck Earth and created an ice age. I don't blame Jeter for being angry with A-Rod—anyone this side of Mother Teresa would have been furious, but after I learned how Jeter behaved when Alex arrived, I'd be lying if I said I wasn't disappointed in Jeter for not acting like a professional. Alex clearly threw the first few punches, but Jeter's subsequent actions were far worse because he let his personal feelings hurt the team. You don't win championships if the team captain infects the clubhouse with hostility. He didn't have to be friends with Alex, but as a teammate, he needed to let go of the past for the good of the club. While this doesn't show up in the box score, Derek made the biggest error of his career when his inability to control his emotions negatively affected the chemistry of the team he was supposed to lead. Jeter was given that responsibility when he accepted the role of team captain. One of CC Sabathia's main concerns about signing with the Yankees was the divided clubhouse. Cashman told CC that he was the kind of man who could bring the team together. Just think of how powerful it could have been if Jeter had forgiven Alex and welcomed him to the Yankees. Who knows what truly great things could have happened.

And such was the tainted climate for most of Hideki Matsui's tenure in the Bronx, yet in spite of all that adversity, Matsui shone with honor, dignity, and drama—the right kind. Even though he had rock-star status in Japan and became a Yankees superstar, I never witnessed an iota of arrogance in him. He nodded to the umpire and the opposing team's catcher when he stepped up to the plate. He didn't showboat, pat himself on the back, or argue balls and strikes. He treated the game with respect, and while he had a tendency to hit that chopper directly into the glove of the second baseman, he, much like Jeter, always seemed to *wow* us at just the right moment. His numbers with the Yankees are impressive: **Years**: 7; **Games**: 916; **Hits**: 977; **Doubles**: 196; **RBI**: 597; **Homers**: 140; **Batting Average**: .292.

Matsui, a two-time All Star and durable workhorse, played 518 consecutive games to begin his MLB career, and he broke the Yankees single-season home run record by a designated hitter, previously held by Don Baylor. While these statistics are admirable, it was Matsui's clutch performances that endeared him to fans and wrote his name into Yankees folklore. Hideki's RBI single against Roy Halladay in Toronto during his first major league at bat was impressive, but his *grand salami* during his first home game at Yankee Stadium happens to be a record.

In the riveting 2003 ALCS Game 7 at Yankee Stadium against Boston, Matsui got up facing Pedro Martinez in the eighth inning with the Yankees losing 5-3. Bernie was on first, Matsui, who had a fourth-inning double off Martinez, worked himself into a two-strike count and then ripped a fastball down the right field line for a ground-rule double. That set the stage for Posada who doubled in Matsui and Williams. This tied the game and set up the historic moment in Yankees-Boston history when Aaron Boone took knuckleballer Tim Wakefield deep in the eleventh inning. It reminded New Yorkers and Bostonians of the Bucky Dent blast in the '78 AL East tie-breaker game at Fenway Park. Without Matsui's big hit, Boone never would have gotten that opportunity. Matsui destroyed Boston in 2009 when he tied Lou Gehrig's record of seven RBI at Fenway Park, a record held since 1930—and he did it Matsui style, crushing two home runs. Two days later Matsui wreaked havoc on Boston again, this time taking Josh Beckett out of the park twice. He also hit a 2009 walk-off home run against Baltimore pitcher Jim Johnson, which tied the Yankees with Boston for first place in the AL East.

No one will ever forget Matsui's annihilation of the Phillies in the 2009 World Series while playing in only three games, because as designated hitter he couldn't play in National League ballparks. Without Hideki, there's a possibility we wouldn't have won that series. After the Yankees lost Game 1 at the Stadium to their foe, Cliff Lee, Matsui took revenge and evened up the series when he stepped up to the plate in the sixth inning with the game knotted at one. Godzilla smashed a 1-2 pitch over the short porch in right for the go-ahead run, and what makes it all the better is that he did it against Pedro Martinez who was now pitching for Philadelphia.

That home run off Pedro was especially satisfying for me, because I have nothing but contempt for Pedro Martinez, and it's not because he was the ace of the Red Sox—it's because he's so damned arrogant! By his own admission, he threw at hitters throughout his career, and he attempted to justify his actions by saying that he retaliated as repayment for his teammates being drilled. That statement is laughable. I'll bet even Red Sox fans had a chuckle over that line. I just can't respect an individual like him. I wasn't surprised when he admitted it—I had assumed that he threw at batters because I watched him pitch so often. Another angle into why I'm not a fan of Martinez's character, or lack of it, is when he slammed then seventy-two year old Don Zimmer to the ground like he was a piece of trash, and it wasn't so much *that* he did it, because Zimmer came at him, it was *how* he did it that sums up Pedro Martinez. It was all there in his nasty expression—his cocky body language. More insight into Martinez can be seen when he was pitching for the Montreal Expos in 1996 and he plunked Philadelphia Phillies Gregg Jefferies in the elbow, and since it happened in the National League, Pedro had to taste his own medicine when he came to bat. When pitcher Mike Williams threw at Pedro, he charged the mound and viciously threw his helmet at Williams before punches began to fly. Yeah, so it is extra gratifying that Matsui humbled Martinez in the 2009 World Series.

Back to Matsui's domination of the Phillies in Game 6. Matsui drove in six of the Yankees' seven runs to clinch number twenty-seven at Yankee

Stadium, and because of his heroics he became the first Japanese player in Major League Baseball to be honored as a World Series MVP. He also tied Bobby Richardson for the most RBI in a World Series game. Albert Pujols joined Richardson and Matsui after driving in six in the 2011 Series. Matsui's numbers for the three games he played in the 2009 World Series are legendary: **Homers**: 3; **Runs Batted In**: 8; **Batting Average**: .615. And for all his World Series accomplishments, for all of his grit, achievements, honor, and dedication, the Yankees disrespected a man who, like Bernie Williams, was entitled to respect. The end of the 2009 World Series was the end of Matsui's contract. He cleared out his locker, and his career with the Yankees was over.

The Yankees felt his fielding ability didn't qualify him as an everyday outfielder, which might have been true, but you don't let a man like that go. Matsui said he loved the Yankees, but he didn't feel valued because when his agent called to negotiate, they offered him *nothing*. Matsui left to play for the Angels in 2010 and signed a one-year, $6.5 million contract, without condemnation or criticism of his former team—no jabs in the media about how the Yankees showed him no respect. If he felt as though the Yankees insulted him, he kept it to himself, which was the professional thing to do. He left New York without compromising his integrity. He also left New York with the love of Yankees fans everywhere.

Matsui had a good year with the Angels in 2010: **Hits**: 132; **Doubles** 24; **Homers**: 21, **Runs Batted In**: 90; **Batting Average**: .274. Like Bernie Williams, Hideki Matsui would have added the stability of a quality veteran presence in the clubhouse. The Yankees did the same asinine thing with Raul Ibanez who was a clutch performer for the Yankees in the 2012 postseason. Ibanez created a record as the first man to hit three home runs in the ninth inning or later in a single postseason game, and they didn't resign him. Doesn't a team that *expects* to be in the postseason every year want to sign players who perform well in the postseason? The Mariners gave Ibanez a one-year $2.75 million contract, and he batted .242 with 29 homers and 65 RBI 124 games. All that for $2.75 million; the Yankees can afford to blow that much on lunch. Yet the Yankees offered Nick Swisher a contract before he signed a much better one with Cleveland—but at least the Yankees offered him something! I liked Swisher; he was always happy and he loved the Bleacher Creatures, but the man was a postseason choke artist. His postseason batting average is .165—86 points off his regular season batting average. Swisher batted .000 in the 2013 wild card game while he was with the Indians. He was up four times and he struck out twice. This is the kind of player who is not a good fit for the Yankees. In fact, I want Swisher on the team we play against in the postseason.

In 2013, the Yankees "honored" Matsui with the little public-relations show they are so good at, by signing him to a one-day minor league contract so he could officially retire as a Yankee. They had a pre-game ceremony, which ensured maximum profits by filling the ballpark to the brim with Matsui fans. I'm sorry, but the Yankees feigned loyalty is despicable. Even if Matsui made the offer to retire as a Yankee, the damage was done when Hideki practically handed them their twenty-seventh championship, and the Yankees never so much as gave him the opportunity to peruse a contract.

Hideki Matsui will live on through the nostalgic discussions of baseball fans for many years to come. Sure, he had his payday, but, like Bernie, when it came down to it, he wanted to play for the Yankees, and he proved it from the beginning when he turned down a six-year $64 million contract at $10.6 million a year from his hometown Yomiuri Giants to play in the Bronx for a three-year $21 million contract at $7 million a year. Those of us who watched Matsui in action will never forget the thrill of this powerful yet humble Yankee superstar. Hey Hideki, I know I speak for many fans when I say that it was an honor watching you play the game.

Stupid Money

The antithesis of Hideki Matsui is Alexander Emmanuel Rodriguez. Both were blessed with superstar talent. Matsui is loved and respected and A-Rod is despised and detested—his legacy tainted in unattractive hues. He's a player who has earned the many sobriquets *Stray-Rod* (caught with a stripper while married), *A-Roid* (steroids), and *A-Fraud* (for getting caught using steroids in 2013 after asking America to forgive him when he was busted for them in 2009). I thought about naming his chapter "Tragic Hero," but A-Rod doesn't fit the criterion; there is no catharsis during his humiliating fall from grace. I almost didn't include anything on A-Rod because what else is there to say, regarding his ignominious story, that's not been said? However A-Rod must have a chapter in a book about how egotism and greed are destroying baseball.

While still a teenager, A-Rod exploded onto the scene during his first tour of duty in the majors with the offensive powerhouse Seattle Mariners, who were managed by "Sweet" Lou Piniella. A-Rod fit nicely in a lineup that featured Ken Griffey Jr., Jay Buhner, Edgar Martinez, and Tino Martinez. It didn't take Alex long before he stood atop the baseball world, as he was young, strong, fast, feared, and respected. A-Rod had extraordinary potential, plus he was having a *bromance* with Derek Jeter—the polished, handsome, boy wonder of baseball. The world was his, and like a young, inexperienced, pop star who implodes before our eyes, A-Rod began his downward spiral with choices spawned from insecurity and greed. When I first heard that Texas signed A-Rod to a ten-year, $252 million deal in 2001, I was thrilled. This was perfect for the Yankees, because his lethal bat and nimble fielding would be wasted on the Rangers since they had no pitching, and investing that kind of money in A-Rod would keep them out of contention. Since Jeter and A-Rod were both apex shortstops, I knew we weren't going to get him, and so his transfer to Texas for ten long years was amazing news! It was a surprise when he signed with the Yankees in 2004, but it didn't seem like a bad idea at the time, especially since he came within a hair of landing somewhere between Manny Ramirez and David Ortiz. Fate, however, placed him at Yankee Stadium where his presence caused the inevitable tsunami.

The collapse of A-Rod's character began with greed, and I wasn't shocked when I heard A-Rod's steroid confession. He said he did PEDs because he needed to prove that he was worth the money and the hype. When you get paid upwards of $26 million a year, people *unrealistically* expect you to hit a home run every time you're up or at least every darn time there's a man on. No one can live up to such standards; however, a player is forgiven when he's a clutch performer. I've seen numerous players fold after getting a huge contract: Joe Mauer, B.J. Upton, Jack McDowell, Johan Santana, and Barry Zito are just a few. Not everyone can handle that kind of pressure. Babe Ruth could do it, as he was paid $80,000 a year in 1930 when a man was happy making $1000 annually, but Ruth, the highest paid ball player of the time, wasn't fazed by pressure. Mickey Mantle (1958 and 1962) and Yogi Berra (1956-57) were the highest paid players of their time, but they performed.

A-Rod needed to *prove to himself* that he was worth it, and that reveals much about his emotional makeup. He might seem cocksure on the outside, but it's evident that his core is fragile. He brought all that extra pressure on himself twice, once with the Rangers, as the highest paid ballplayer in history, and again with the Yankees who were *insane* for giving him, at thirty- two-years old, a ten year $275 million contract, which again made Alex the highest paid baseball player at that time. Although using steroids in 2009, A-Rod carried the Yankees through the playoffs before becoming human again and handing the baton to Matsui for the World Series.

A-Rod provided one of my greatest experiences at Yankee Stadium during Game 2 of the 2009 ALDS against the Minnesota Twins. Even though the Yankees were down three to one in the bottom of the ninth, I was confident that we were coming back because the Stadium vibe felt and like a pack of '68 Dodge Chargers revving hotter and louder as the innings waned in the sharp-white light of Yankee Stadium at night. The more we breathed in that fiery Bronx air the more pumped up we became; we were feeding off each other's adrenaline. Mark Teixeira's ninth-inning single spiked a power surge of raucous cheers, but A-Rod's 3-1 ninth-inning home run, which crash landed a few feet from where my son and I were sitting in the right-field bleachers, sent Yankee Stadium into a raging frenzy. I'm not a Bleacher Creature in the true sense of the word, because I don't go to every Yankees game like a true Creature does, but I haven't sat anywhere but the bleachers for the past twenty years. Love him or hate him, A-Rod delivered big in 2009—but that was pretty much it for Alex, *clutch-wise*, until the pleasant surprise of 2015; however, that bubble burst midway through the season when he ran out of gas.

I'll bet A-Rod's story would have had a much happier ending if he hadn't signed those immodest contracts. If he signed for millions less—even a hundred million less—he still would have made over a hundred million dollars. Signing for fewer millions would have removed him from the epicenter of the relentless spotlight that skewered him throughout his career. Maybe without that pressure he would never have done steroids, and I believe his stats would have been Hall of Fame worthy without PEDs. Many of you may be thinking:

> *So big frigging deal if he's not liked! He's rich, famous, and he dates fashion models and movie stars!*

While that may be true, I believe he would have had all those perks anyway, and now he's lost his reputation. He's joined Roger, Mark, Barry, Sammy, and the growing list of baseball pariahs. He has to live in his skin for the rest of his life, as a cheater, a choker, an overpaid has-been who will always be defending his tainted stats and bearing the brunt of criticism. Isn't it better to sleep at night feeling good about yourself, proud of your accomplishments, knowing you're respected? Sleeping like **Monseigneur Bienvenu* is worth millions; the payoff isn't cash, it's peace of mind.

One of the problems with human beings is that we *think* we can buy anything. We fool ourselves into thinking that money is the *cure-all*, but money can't make problems disappear or buy peace of mind. If money accomplished this, all lottery winners would he happy, and they're not. After the initial euphoria diminishes, their life is their life. There are many winners of the big prize who wish they'd never played the game.

Andrew "Jack" Whittaker hit for $315 million and began buying expensive toys, gambling, drinking, and frequenting strip clubs. He was repeatedly robbed, his daughter died (money couldn't prevent that), his granddaughter and her boyfriend abused drugs and died three months apart, and the boyfriend was found dead in Whittaker's home. Whittaker sobbed to reporters, at the time of his daughter's death, that he wished he'd ripped up the ticket. Andrew "Jack" Whittaker was broke four years after his "lucky" pay day.

When Billie Bob Harrell Jr. won $31 million he quit his job, invested in fruitless enterprises, and donated lots of money to charities, but then he became inundated with calls from strangers demanding donations. Harrell also suffered in his personal life as well; he committed suicide in his home by way of a shotgun blast. He is alleged to have said winning the lottery was the worst thing that ever happened to him.

William Post III won $16.2 million and was broke three months later. Besides reckless spending and being conned, his own brother was arrested for hiring a hit man to kill Post and his wife! William Post died of respiratory disease at the age of sixty-six.

Sixteen-year-old Callie Rogers hit for $3 million and six years later she was bankrupt. That six-year spending frenzy was a cocktail of reckless living, cars, homes, parties, and two attempted suicides. After she blew through the money, she moved in with her mother and worked as a cleaning lady.

Is A-Rod much different? Yeah, he hit the biggest baseball lottery of all time… twice, but what did it buy him? Did it make him happy? Perhaps at times, but I doubt he's satisfied or content. Did it cause him extreme stress and anxiety? Yes, it did. Did it cause unrealistic expectations from fans? Yes it did. Did it instigate steroid use? Yes it did. Did the factors surrounding the money, ego, and steroids create a negative persona for the once respected elite shortstop? Absolutely. Will the steroids make him ill? Perhaps, as they are suspected of causing tumors, heart and circulatory issues, liver abnormalities, tendon rupture, prostate enlargement, rage, and depression. Intimidating NFL defensive end Lyle Alzado believed steroids caused the inoperable brain tumor that, painfully, ended his life at the age of forty-three. Alzado's last wish was that nobody should ever die the way he did. Is A-Rod happy with the legacy he has shaped? Who knows, but he has all that money, right?

**Monseigneur Bienvenu is a character from Les Misérables whose conscience is so clear–his character so pure–he sleeps in a state of profound peace and tranquility.*

Rundown

While Paul O'Neill's lifetime pro baseball salary of $51.6 million was meager by the standards of his Yankee teammates (Bernie Williams, $103 million; Jorge Posada, $117 million; Mariano Rivera; $169 million; Derek Jeter, $265 million), he was, however, not underpaid. O'Neill made more than $50 million over the course of his celebrated career. Even if he made $75 million it wouldn't have been excessive for what he brought to the game, and I'm saying this about Paul O'Neill, a man I believe was the best player of the last dynasty. Jeter might have been the face of the team, but O'Neill was the spine, heart, and soul.

As I'm writing this book, the Yankees signed Chase Headley to a four-year $52 million contract with incentives that could raise it to $14 million per year. In 2014 Headley was a good fielder who batted .243, drove in a meager 49 RBI, and hit 13 home runs. In four years Headley will make more money than O'Neill made over the course of his entire career. I realize that O'Neill retired in 2001, but it's not like O'Neill retired in the 1980s. I surmise that Chase Headley, by the time he retires, will make double what Paul O'Neill made. No offense to Headley because he might be a great guy, but as a ballplayer he couldn't carry O'Neill's cleats. When a player with Chase Headley's abilities stands to make $100 million over the course of his career, there is something very wrong, and it needs to be fixed.

Inordinate salaries place pressure on the system, and it's reckless. The alarming part is that fans keep shelling out for it. When will we stop? Where does it end? We just complain and hand over the plastic. The prices of official Yankees jerseys on MLB.com hover around $200.00, and yet we keep buying them. How about players who charge fans for their autographs? I know that autographs have become a business and some people sell autographs on eBay, but big frigging deal! You, the ballplayer making millions and millions, are worried that some autograph recipients are selling your *sacred* penmanship for a few bucks? Have you considered the psyched fan who just wants to display a baseball or a bat that you "graced" with your signature? Does everything have to come down to money? It's shameful that multimillionaires charge fans for their autographs. It may not even be a kid, it may be an adult who admires your skills—someone who respects you. If no one bought players' memorabilia, you'd see how fast that nonsense would end.

Outrageous salaries are a huge part of what's wrong with this sport, and there's no end in sight. If we want balance in professional baseball, fans need to pledge allegiance to each other; if we do that, change will occur. This book provides a place and a plan to make this change possible. What begins with us will spread across baseball and beyond.

PART 4

Hank, Hal, Brian, Joe, and George

• • •

"He who is not contented with what he has, would not be contented with what he would like to have."

~ Socrates

• • •

Paradise Lost

In the previous section I compared players poisoned by greed, ego, and pride and those who maintained their dignity amidst the tornado of money swirling throughout pro baseball. Joe Torre wasn't affected by dollars so much, but his pride and ego wrote a sad chapter at the end of a mostly magical career as manager of the New York Yankees. What happened between Joe Torre and the Yankees is most unfortunate, and its theme is found in literature throughout the ages. John Milton's *Paradise Lost*, teaches that excessive pride is perilous. Lucifer, the most magnificent of all angels, fell from grace because of it. Milton recognized that pride is detrimental to coexistence. Whether it's between God and angels or between one person and another, pride generates conflict.

We knew that there was animosity between Joe Torre and the New York Yankees after they parted ways in 2008, but the gravity of Torre's "fall from grace" was written in enormous block letters across every electronic screen at the closing ceremony of the old Yankee Stadium, on September 21, 2008, by the *omission* of his image during the videos illustrating the Yankees' majestic history. The Yankees simply *erased* Joe Torre.

Should the Yankees have honored Torre? On a professional level, yes, they should have, as you cannot expunge the contributions of a manager who led your team to twelve postseason appearances and four World Championships in twelve years. Perhaps the Yankees, like the political leaders in Shakespeare's *Julius Caesar*, feared the fickle crowd. Seeing larger-than-life footage of Joe Torre accepting a World Series trophy… or four, might have given rise to another "Steinbrenner sucks" chant that rocked Yankee Stadium after Reggie Jackson hit a home run in his return to the

Bronx in 1982 after George didn't sign him in 1981. Steinbrenner's stinging memory of that infamous chant may have been the reason why Joe Torre was stricken from Yankees history at the ballpark's closing ceremony. Whatever the reason, it was ugly and a result of pride and ego—on both sides.

I loved Joe Torre as a manager and respect the fact that he won four World Series in five years, but he was wrong to call the Yankees 2008 contract offer (a one-year-major-league leading $5 million deal, with the possibility of another $3 million in incentives) an "insult." Torre's previous contract wasn't performance-based, so there was a possibility that he would have made less money in 2008 if the Yankees didn't do well in the postseason. Shortly after turning down the one-year deal, Torre stated that the Yankees made him an offer that he *had* to refuse. In saying this Torre admits that this incentive-laden contract was a blow to his pride and ego. You could argue that the Yankees were playing politics and wanted to explore managerial options other than Torre, but, whatever their reasons, they offered him a lucrative contract. If Torre thought it was an insult, he should simply have refused it, as he did, and moved on, which he didn't. His playing the victim was not dignified; his grumbling to the press burnt the bridge between him and the closing ceremony of Yankee Stadium.

Torre had a historic run with the Yankees, but the magic was gone several years prior to 2008, and he, like many successful sports figures, couldn't tell when it was time to retire. The list is long, but a few notables such as Michael Jordan, Patrick Ewing, Muhammad Ali, Sugar Ray Leonard, Roger Clemens, Steve Carlton, Brett Favre, and soccer legend Pelé, demonstrate how once elite sports figures should have stepped down sooner.

While the Yankees were cleaning out their lockers at the end of September in 2008, Joe Torre's Dodgers were gearing up for October baseball, but does anyone believe the Yankees would have made it into the postseason with Torre managing? Besides, Torre didn't take a floundering team into the playoffs; he took a heavily salaried Dodgers team and did with them what he'd done with the Yankees during his final years in pinstripes: The Dodgers were the 2008 winners of the NLDS (3-0) and were the losers of the 2008 NLCS (4-1). Torre had the exact postseason record with the Dodgers in 2009, and in 2010 his team finished the season with a losing record.

Joe Torre had done all that he could do with the Yankees. He was the right man at the right time in 1996, but after winning for so long, he lost his *mojo*. There's no fault in this—it just happens. The Yanks got soft under Torre, as he was playing gentleman's ball against a pack of hungry wolves, and, yes, I'm talking about the Boston Red Sox. It was like in *Rocky III* when Rocky was preparing for the big fight in his expensive gym with all the luxuries winning provides, but the camera jumped to a raw, sweaty Clubber Lang, and the audience knew that Rocky had no chance against this younger, hungrier foe.

Boston pitchers were *drilling* our guys without retaliation. I'm not suggesting that it's appropriate for pitchers to throw at batters in order to gain an advantage, but if you don't pay it forward, it's open season on your own guys, and that's how you lose games. In the 2004 ALCS, Boston pitchers hit *seven* Yankee batters, and Yankee pitchers hit *one* Red Sox batter (probably an errant pitch); and what's not listed in the box score were the near hits—the high and tights, especially from Pedro. Matsui wasn't hit, but he had a few close calls, and he looked tentative from Game 4 on. He went 9-15 in the first three games and 5-19 in the last four games. I remember saying that Matsui looked scared at the plate. The Yankees batters looked intimidated, but Red Sox hitters were standing at the plate with swagger. Joe Torre was watching this happen, and he continued his gentleman's game—a philosophy that played a crucial role in the Red Sox' degradation of the Yankees. Torre should have told his guys that every time a Boston pitcher hits one of ours, we hit one of theirs, and to let fly with high and tights, because when you're truly hungry—ravenous—you're not overly concerned with being a gentleman; that's a risk you take in the heat of battle. Torre could afford to preserve his proper decorum because he had four rings, so the burn to win a fifth was obviously there, but it was more of a want than a need. Joe Torre no longer had the wherewithal to lead his team to victory after they were up 3-0 in the ALCS in 2004 against their bitter rivals, and that infamous defeat concluded with the sickening scene of the Red Sox celebrating inside the Great Ballpark in the Bronx—dancing on its infield in front of its home fans with the legends of Monument Park in the background.

The tide turned between the Yankees and Red Sox with Joe Torre as manager; it happened on *his* watch. Joe Torre was no longer that guy who, after losing Game 1 against Atlanta in 1996, responded to George Steinbrenner's Game 2 "must-win" command, by telling George not to expect much against Greg Maddux that night, but that they would go to Atlanta where they would sweep the Braves in their own park and then win it all at Yankee Stadium. That's fire! That's chutzpah! Terry "Tito" Francona became the man Torre had been—the man who could follow through on a bold statement, and I'll never forget the moment the words flew from Tito's mouth. Although I combed the Net searching for the post-game press conference on October 16, 2004, I couldn't access it, so I can't quote his exact words but he ended with something like *I'll see you at Yankee Stadium* or *I'll see you tomorrow*, just as he turned and walked away. He said it in a way that asserted, this series is *not* over! He looked pissed, confident, resolute—ready to fight—ready for war. The metaphoric gloves fell to the ground as he walked away. *That* was the moment of the role reversal between the Red Sox and the Yankees, and I'm not saying that this debacle was all Torre's doing, as there were obviously other factors involved, but Joe Torre has major ownership in this. It wasn't so bad that the Red Sox broke the Curse of the Bambino, it was *how* and *where* Boston gave it to us, which resulted in the everlasting trivia question of disgrace. The 2004 ALCS made up for at least the Bucky Dent and Aaron Boone home runs combined. Since 2004, the Boston Red Sox are undoubtedly the better team; their three rings (2004, 2007, 2013) to our one (2009) proves it. 2004 turned the tide, and I never thought I would see it happen, but it sure as hell did.

Another factor of this reversal was Mo; Boston hitters beat the greatest closer in the history of baseball, yet I don't blame Rivera. Mariano was overused and the Sox were able to get to him; he, the greatest of all time, didn't have the goods to stop them because of all those two-inning saves. If Mariano had not been spent, he might not have been manhandled like he was. Joe overworked his pitchers by using a fluke model that went by the wayside after the magic of Nelson, Stanton, and Rivera. Joe kept relying on a strategy that worked well with those guys for a few years, but when Stanton and Nelson were gone, he kept trying to continue something that was no longer available. Joe Torre's indiscriminate use of Scott Proctor, Steve Karsay, Tom Gordon, Paul Quantrill, Tanyon Sturtze, Kyle Farnsworth, and even Marino Rivera ruined some careers (obviously not Rivera's).

As the Yankees tossed around the idea of extending Joe Torre's tenure, I'm sure these matters were discussed. The Yankees knew they were spending a lot of money building a team around a core of elite players, but Torre, with a talent-laden-championship team, kept falling short. Moreover, Torre took his flawed bullpen philosophy to the Dodgers, as he burned out Cory Wade's young arm and overworked closer Jonathan Broxton, righty Ramon Troncoso, and lefty George Sherrill. It's been suggested that Torre overused Russell Martin into a hip injury when Martin was a young pup with the Dodgers. Again, making it to the postseason is notable, but if your team repeatedly goes down early, something is wrong.

Even Terry Francona needed to leave Boston after all his success. His time came and went. He was the right man to lead the Boston Red Sox through the land mines of the Bambino Curse to beat the Yankees and become World Champions, but he lost his ability to control the free-spirited, long-haired, bearded boys of Beantown. Even though Francona didn't win as many rings as Torre, his accomplishments are just as lofty because under his leadership he instilled respect for a team with a long history of being deemed losers—under him, they changed the Yankees-Red Sox paradigm and helped make Boston a force to be reckoned with.

Finally, Torre's fierce loyalty to certain players reveals flawed leadership. There are reports that Torre added fuel to the tense clubhouse atmosphere during the Jeter-Rodriguez conflict, because Joe would have no problem reaming Alex, but Jeter could do no wrong. It seems crystal clear that A-Rod was intimidated by the revered captain and the veteran manager. Torre needed to end Jeter's nonsense. The reason why I believe what's said about Torre in the A-Rod matter is because whenever I saw Torre speak of Jeter, his face changed; he lit up. Jeter was *very* special in Torre's eyes—the favorite child. Jeter referred to Torre as a second father. That being the case, Torre might have been the only one to make Jeter see the damage he was causing to the team and how the Captain needed to forgive his former friend. Torre, feeling as he did about Jeter, may have taken A-Rod's past media jabs at Jeter, personally, the way one rallies around a friend who has been wronged. Torre seemed to have had his favorites, and A-Rod didn't appear to have been part of that select group… I don't believe Shane Spencer made it to the short list either.

I remember when Shane Spencer exploded onto the scene in September 1998 hitting ten home runs, including three grand slams, in only sixty-seven at bats. He became the star of the team, and the media ate it up. It was like Shane Spencer flew in from Krypton. Even though Shane was lighting up New York, Joe Torre didn't wrap his arms around the kid when asked about him by the press; it seemed that he downplayed Spencer's heroics. I remember thinking that Torre wasn't very fond of the new star, even though Shane injected life into a team that was floundering at the end of the historic 1998 season (between 8/19/98 and 9/19/98 the Yankees were 15-17). Perhaps Torre felt that Spencer was going to be the *one-hit-wonder* he turned out to be—or perhaps Torre's unenthusiastic tone displayed a window into some kind of loyalty issue because this rookie was stealing the spotlight from his mainstay players. Joe Torre once said that he must be loyal to a whole team, as opposed to one player on a team. He was obviously aware of a solid managerial philosophy, but, ironically, his fervid commitment to some of his favorite players prevented him from following that credo.

Joe Torre, one of the greatest managers in baseball history, had flaws, and there's no insult in that because we all have weaknesses. The one-year-major-league-leading $5 million contract offered to him by the Yankees was no insult. It was time for Joe to move on. Torre's bullpen plan worked flawlessly through 2000, his loyalty to the players may have galvanized the team through 2000, and some luck may have come his way through 2000, but pride and ego tainted the relationship between him and the Yankees.

I realize that there was a political mending between the Yankees and Torre in 2014 when they retired his No. 6 and gave him a plaque in Monument Park, but it's like the breakup of any relationship: mistakes were made and things are never quite the same.

Easy Street

How lucky is Brian Cashman? As general manager of the New York Yankees, he gets to search the planet for baseball talent with a sack of money over each shoulder, and the best part is that it's not his money and he's not held accountable for it. The Yankees, under Cashman, have squandered huge sums of cash on players who are either *at* or just *beyond* their peak, and the "Cash Man" signs many of them to illogical, over moneyed, multi-year deals with opt-out clauses. The man is a dinosaur; his philosophy worked when the Yankees had a team built on the solid foundation of young homegrown studs: Derek Jeter, Andy Pettitte, Jorge Posada, Mariano Rivera, Bernie Williams, and Ramiro Mendoza (who pitched for Boston after the Yankees let him go). With this pool of in-house talent, the Yankees could buy the few big pieces to complete the puzzle.

It's either Brian Cashman hasn't figured out that trying to buy a team of aging stars doesn't work, or he's grown too comfortable. George Steinbrenner tried to buy championships, a strategy which worked initially when free agency was in its infancy, but then failed miserably as he spent exorbitant amounts of money on once-great players while trading away cheap, young talent. During that period, the Yankees went thirteen years, 1982-94, without playing October baseball. Winning a World Championship will remain just beyond the reach of the present Yankees if the combination of Cashman and the Steinbrenner brothers continues. Second place finishes, one-game playoffs, and early exits to the off season will remain the norm. Hank and Hal can hold themselves harmless and say they've spent tons of money trying to build a World Series team for New York, and one look at the Yankees' payroll proves that they've spent. My question is, do Hank and Hal really care all that much about winning the World Series?

Of course the Steinbrenner brothers would *like* to win, but I question their hearts in the same way I question Robinson Cano's. Their old man had a *voracious* appetite for winning, but I don't see a shadow of that hunger in either of George's boys. Even with the failing teams of late, Hank and Hal grow wealthier by the year. The Steinbrenner money belt grows in tandem with the ever-expanding obese Yankees waistline, and it is *we* who are their benefactors—Hank and Hal do not contribute one penny to the pot! Fans are responsible for the funds that the Steinbrenners appropriate to both themselves and to building the team. One of the problems is that there is so much cash available that after a bad deal or a bad year, Cashman needs only to lower the money bucket into the deep Bronx well, which never runs dry for the New York Yankees.

The prevailing Yankees leadership seems content with the "spend-to-win" concept, yet teams like the A's, Rays, Royals, Orioles, and Indians prove that you don't need a $200 million payroll to be successful. However, Hank and Hal signed Brian Cashman, of the Jurassic Period, to a three year contract extension in 2014 even though the Yankees hadn't made it into the playoffs for two consecutive years. 2015 was interesting, as the Yankees backed into a playoff spot because of their excellent first half; however, A-Rod, Teixeira, and Sabathia, an investment of over $68 million, were basically nonexistent the second half of the year. It's clear that the Yankees will swim in mediocrity until they stop offering long egregious contracts to players whose best years are behind them.

Cashman showed restraint in 2015 as he held onto some good rookies at the trade deadline, and I'm not yet sure if it's the propaganda he spreads through the media regarding "untouchable" rookies or if it's something else. Whatever the reason, mediocrity hasn't been so rough on the Steinbrenners, as streams of money flood their enormous cups, and Brian Cashman is there to squeegee the excess into the gutters along 161st Street.

Comedy Tragedy

George Steinbrenner was theatre—pure entertainment from the get-go. He was a character from *commedia dell'arte*, vaudeville, the villain in a Steven Seagal film, or the antagonist of a television sitcom. And while he wasn't a man who intended to be funny, the fact that he took everything so seriously made him hilarious at times. The Dave Winfield "Mr. May" quip was insensitive, but one has to admit that it was a pretty funny one-liner. His larger than life frame, expressions and antics gave rise to Bill Gallo's ingenious caricature, General Von Steingrabber. Another bit of genius in its own right is the George Steinbrenner character on *Seinfeld*, and pairing him with George Costanza is the perfect marriage.

I loved the *Seinfeld* episodes featuring Steinbrenner. Here are a few of my favorites: Costanza is sleeping under his desk and Steinbrenner is waiting for Costanza in Costanza's office for three hours, and then Steinbrenner's grandkids come by and Jerry, at Costanza's request, calls in a bomb threat to get Steinbrenner out of the office. This backfires because Steinbrenner orders the kids to get under the desk for protection. Another great one is when Costanza is thought to be dead and Jerry Stiller, Costanza's father, starts yelling at Steinbrenner for trading Jay Buhner. How about when Costanza gets Steinbrenner hooked on eggplant calzones and Costanza gets banned from the pizzeria because the owner thinks he is stealing from the tips jar? Even George Steinbrenner got a kick out of *Seinfeld's* Steinbrenner character; he thought it was a good depiction.

Any way you slice it, George was quite a character. I loved the Yankees' principal owner with the same passion as the rival fans who loathed him. Even if the haters couldn't admit it, they wished they had someone with half of George's inherent need to win. George said that winning comes after breathing. What other team ever had an owner like Steinbrenner? None, and they never will… nor will we. There are some who think that

George Steinbrenner was more of a curse than a savior. They say the only reason the last dynasty emerged was because George was banned from baseball while Gene Michael sowed the seeds that grew into the legacy with which George has become associated. While Gene Michael was running the show, the Yankees assembled the "Core Four" and traded for Paul O'Neill. There would have been no dynasty without those moves. However, the creation of that dynasty was a marriage. George provided the money to build around the nucleus created by Gene Michael, and even though Steinbrenner was absent from day-to-day control, you can bet your life that his presence loomed large; it was still his team and everyone knew it. George was able to fill in the blanks when he returned, and his tireless motivation to win continued the journey that began with Michael's instincts.

The antithesis of George Steinbrenner are Hank and Hal. George was as vibrant as they are colorless. Yet it's unfair to juxtapose George and his sons, because, quite frankly, no one (or two in this case) could've filled the big man's shoes. With George, I always felt that we had a chance. He is synonymous with the famous plaque prominently displayed on his desk: **Lead, follow, or get the hell out of the way.** That adage is George Steinbrenner in ten words, and the following passages demonstrate Steinbrenner's unique leadership style.

After winning the first two games to the Dodgers in the 1981World Series and losing the next four, Steinbrenner issued a public apology to the City of New York for his team's meltdown. His reaction drew criticism, but I admire his stratospheric expectations. Yet the man who apologized for losing the '81 World Series flew the whole team to Thurman Munson's funeral in Ohio even though they had a nationally televised game that night. When a reporter asked George what would happen if they didn't make it back in time for the game, Steinbrenner's response was that his team would forfeit.

His personal handling of the Reggie Jackson negotiations by both wining and dining him at the 21 Club while showcasing him around the streets of New York so people would cheer Reggie on, stroke his ego, and make him want to play here, brought us a legitimate superstar. What would the 1977-78 Yankees have been without Reggie Jackson?

Have you heard about the first time Lou Piniella met George Steinbrenner? Lou was excited to play for the Yankees after he was traded to them in 1973, but when he got to his locker on the first day of spring training, there was no uniform in there. The equipment manager told Piniella that Steinbrenner wanted to see him. Lou went up to George's office, introduced himself, and told him how happy he was to be playing for the Yankees. Steinbrenner told Lou that he was happy he was playing for the Yankees but that his hair was too long. Piniella told George that Jesus was the greatest person who ever lived and he had long hair. Without saying a word, Steinbrenner led Piniella across the road to a swimming pool. George, pointing at the pool, told Lou that if he could walk across the water he could wear his hair any way he wanted. That's classic Steinbrenner!

You also have to admire Steinbrenner's role in forming the Yankees Entertainment & Sports Network. The YES Network was a stroke of genius, as it gave the Yankees media control and a ton of revenue. There was more to George Steinbrenner than his association with the Yankees. He received the Gold Medal Award (the most esteemed award bestowed by the College Football Foundation) for a lifetime of dedication and achievement in both business and personal matters. He supported the United States Olympic Committee for many years, and he was a man with a big heart, a philanthropist who didn't flaunt his abundant generosity. He gave to people and causes because it was part of who he was, and he once said that if a person does a good deed and more than the two people involved know about it, then the good deed was done for the wrong reason.

George was a man who took chances on people, such as Darryl Strawberry, Dwight "Doc" Gooden, and Joe Pepitone. George received a letter from Joe Pepitone's wife, after the couple had fallen on hard times due to Joe's bad choices. Steinbrenner gave him a job as at traveling instructor for the minor leagues, and soon after that he was a hitting instructor for the Yankees. Doc Gooden said that George was like a second father whom he loved and respected because the Boss took an interest in his personal life—George gave him a chance when most people had turned their backs on him. Darryl Strawberry said that people didn't know how much George really cared about others. Steinbrenner taught Darryl to be a fighter, a winner—to never quit. And when Darryl went down hard and had difficulty getting up, George was the one who was there for him. Darryl said George Steinbrenner was like the father he never had.

I always felt that George Steinbrenner was genuine, which was why I wrote to him after the 2004 Red Sox blunder. The letter expressed my angst, and I even gave him some suggestions on what to do with the team—funny when I think of it now. . . I overnighted the letter to two locations: Yankee Stadium in the Bronx and Legends Field in Tampa. I didn't expect a response, but I wasn't surprised when a letter arrived on Yankees stationary. The envelope is from the Bronx as the return address is printed as follows: **Yankee Stadium 161st Street & River Avenue, Bronx, New York 10451**. The envelope, however, is stamped from zip code 33614, and the stationary letterhead reads: **Tampa Office, Legends Field, 1 Steinbrenner Drive, Tampa, Florida 33614 (813) 281-9001**, which means he received my letter in Tampa. Steinbrenner's typed response dated December 1, 2004, said that he understood my disappointment and frustration, and that while the ending of the 2004 season couldn't be changed, the organization would make the necessary changes so that this experience would never happen again. He ended by saying that he was grateful that I wrote to him and that he and his team would do everything they can to bring me and the city of New York another World Championship, because without fans there is no reason to have a Yankees baseball team. George signed this letter with a blue felt pen that bled through the page.

My gut tells me that the Boss would take the time to write a letter to a distraught, loyal fan. In all likelihood there were baskets of letters from disconcerted fans after what happened in '04, and I truly believe he would have answered them, even if he dictated a form letter to his secretary and then signed each one. I believe he would think he owed it to me… to all of us, because he (as in the 1981 World Series) felt as though *he* let us down and that it was his responsibility to acknowledge the fans. I also take into account that my letter was addressed to George Steinbrenner himself, and even if George got letters all the time, this was a year that must have eaten at him. His healing process may have been tied to responding to those letters—it was a direct connection to Yankees fans, something we were experiencing together.

Am I just being a fan? Not sure; this is my gut impression after observing him for thirty-seven years. He wasn't afraid to speak his mind, and he never apologized for weeping in the midst of champagne showers during a World Championship celebration as he was handed the trophy—the ultimate symbol of success. Touching that trophy was pure bliss for him, even if it was short-lived. He admitted that he couldn't enjoy it for very long because he had to start thinking about the next one.

There is a part of me that wants to think that maybe he read my letter and answered it plain and simple; there happens to be one typo in there (it says "an" instead of "and"), which makes me think there's a shot that it's an original. Either way you slice it, it was cool to be acknowledged by the iconic Yankees owner.

There were several facets to George Steinbrenner, and while I featured more of the comedic elements, there are two masks in theatre, and tragedy completes the theatrical emblem. George Steinbrenner was New York's savior and demon, its comedy and its tragedy. He bought the club at a time when the Yankees were playing like an expansion team—a time when the Mets were the *top dog* in town, as they significantly outdrew the Yankees after 1964. Video footage of Yankee Stadium during those anomalous years reveals vast empty patches of vacant blue seats; it was like a Yankees horror film. Being born in 1960, I didn't remember the 1964 World Championship, so my fellow Yankees fans and I only heard stories about the great teams of yesteryear. We were perpetually on the defensive as cocky Mets fans reminded us who the better team was. Our only retort was that our team held the record for the most World Championships, which was a pretty lame response. That was, of course, until Steinbrenner bought the team, restored the universe to its proper alignment, and became a god for a little while before his tomfoolery turned the Yankees into a media circus.

Dick Howser compiled a 103 and 59 record in the regular season in 1980, but losing three straight to the Royals in the American League Championship Series that year proved to Steinbrenner (and possibly Steinbrenner alone) that Howser didn't have what it took to win—a philosophy that was proven wrong five years later when Howser's Royals won the World Series. Gene Michael managed the Yankees after Howser, but in September, 1981 George fired Gene Michael and replaced him with Bob Lemon for the 1982 season. George asserted that under no circumstances would he change managers that year, but after the first fourteen games he fired Bob Lemon and rehired Gene Michael. He went on to fire Michael after a hundred games because of a horrendous showing in the Bronx when the Yankees lost a doubleheader during which righty George Frazier gave up ten runs in 1 and 1/3 innings. Steinbrenner ordered Bob Sheppard to announce that Yankees fans could exchange that night's ticket for a future game. Soon after that, George replaced Gene Michael with Clyde King.

George Steinbrenner was at times like a mad-clown-puppet master who turned the Yankees into a laughing-stock, as he made respectable people dance on the ends of his strings no matter how idiotic he or they looked. Yogi Berra lasted only seventeen games in 1985 after George had given him a guarantee—yes another one—that Yogi would remain the skipper for the full season. What made matters worse was that Steinbrenner didn't deliver the bad news to Berra; he informed Berra through general manager, and former manager, Clyde King who wasn't a stranger to the revolving-manager spectacle. Berra, a man who spent a lifetime building a respectable reputation, would not endure that kind of indignity, and, as we all came to know, vowed to never step foot inside Yankee Stadium as long as Steinbrenner was running the team, and he didn't come back until an older, wiser, and humbled George Steinbrenner apologized nearly fifteen years later.

While firing Yogi humiliated the Yankees organization and soiled the relationship between the Yankees and one of its most beloved icons, it was the hirings and firings of Billy Martin that remained the main feature of Steinbrenner's three-ring circus. Billy went from revered leader to George's court jester. I originally loved that Billy Martin was manager of the Yankees, but as the years went on I couldn't understand why he withstood the humiliation of being hired and fired five times. Especially since it was plastered across newspapers, discussed on TV, and made into beer commercials. It was tough to watch, and sources say there was a sixth round in the works before Billy Martin was killed in an auto accident on Christmas day in 1989. All in all George changed managers twenty times in his first twenty-three seasons, and hired eleven general managers over a thirty-year period. Billy Martin, the other managers, the coaches, the general managers, and the players were all just fodder for Steinbrenner. He would chew them up and spit them back out in the grand scheme of creating a World Championship club; the names and faces were only details; if his chosen individuals failed, he'd simply try others.

Steinbrenner's enigmatic behavior created the atmosphere of Sparky Lyle's, *The Bronx Zoo*, a tell-all book revealing the lunacy of the volatile club which grew from Steinbrenner's controversial leadership. The apropos nickname adhered to the Yankees right through the eighties. Steinbrenner's boisterous passion and unrealistic demands turned him into a caricature, as he tried to win the World Series with the best club money could buy. He kept putting good teams on the field, but not World Championship teams, so he fired, hired, ranted, and exploded all over the media. It is said that he even fired a secretary for not bringing him a tuna sandwich on whole wheat bread. There was also the Dave Winfield mess, where the Boss, believing Winfield outsmarted him in their contract negotiations, hired a man named Howard Spira to dig up dirt on Winfield. The result was Steinbrenner's "permanent" banishment from day-to-day management, but not team ownership of the Yankees.

We loved George Steinbrenner because he tried his best to win it all every year, and while he appeared so much larger than life, he was so very human, and with George, everything was big. His heart was big, his persona was big, and so were his mistakes.

George once admitted that he hasn't always done a great job, but that he always tried—and that's the reason why I've forgive him for the biggest debacle in Yankees history…

King George

George Steinbrenner did much for the Yankees organization, but his overzealous nature, his keen financial aptitude, and above all, his unimpeded ego took a chunk out of the bond between the Yankees and their fans, and it happened with one single decision. Steinbrenner claims to have been entrusted with a tradition, which he crushed, gutted, and stole from us—its rightful heirs. The tradition with which he was entrusted, belongs to us, not him. He stole it when he forced the Yankees and their fans out of Yankee Stadium on East 161st Street & River Avenue and built that soulless structure on 1 East 161st Street. Was ego the driving force behind George's decision? You bet it was! How powerful was it for him to know that he, George Michael Steinbrenner III, was responsible for rewriting Yankees history and building a new Yankee Stadium? *King* George's name is now synonymous with the Yankees in a way that transcends what it had been. His name, good or bad, will be linked with the Yankees for as long as that building stands. With a price tag of roughly $1.5 billion, the marriage between *Steinbrenner Stadium, New York* and the Yankees will continue for as long as the Yankees exist, as it was he who both masterminded and executed the deal.

There was nothing architecturally wrong with The House that Ruth Built, as it was deemed safe in 2001 by structural engineer Antranig Ouzoonian—even though the Yankees originally tried to sell that "structurally unsafe" garbage prior to its official evaluation by Ouzoonian.

Ouzoonian pronounced that Yankee Stadium wasn't just spruced up in 1975, it had been structurally renovated.

It really came down to money and power. The Stadium, according to the Yankees, lacked the financial benefits of newer stadiums; however, the old ballpark would have been more lucrative in the end, because of its energy, fan base, and history. The deflated energy at *Steinbrenner Stadium, New York*, cannot compare to the passion and palpable decibel volume of East 161st Street & River Avenue, and I believe that the decline in passion will lead to a less loyal and less enthusiastic fan base—a declining "fannies in the seats" (as Steinbrenner used to say) fan base—which may cause fewer titles because the bond between us and them has been compromised. East 161st Street and River Avenue had baseball's roots pressed into its playing field. That building was a museum; not at all like the pitiful museum at the new place, but an archeological treasure where the heroes of baseball resided, fought, and sweated their way into legend.

Money cannot create the mystique and presence of that arena. The bottom line cannot recreate what has become extinct—the nostalgia of baseball. Money cannot rekindle the sounds of history, twenty-six World Championships, or Lou Gehrig's poignant final words. Will Lou Gehrig ever walk onto a baseball field again? Joe DiMaggio? Mickey Mantle? Will the Babe? Who will replace them? Who can? Will there ever be another historic Murderers' Row? Will the dynasties of the 1920s, 1930s, 1940s, 1950s, 1960s, and the late 1990's to 2000s ever walk on the soil of *Steinbrenner Stadium, New York*? It was George Steinbrenner who washed his hands of East 161st Street and River Avenue and drove the nails into its coffin. He abandoned that shrine, and we were forced to watch it happen. We were forced to leave it too. How arrogant was he to think that he had that right? Yes, he had the say because he had the money and the power, but he didn't have the right. He didn't consult the fans. You might be thinking:

Why would the principal owner of the New York Yankees have to ask?

The answer is simply that he owed it to us. You know, the ones he claimed were the basis for just about everything! The ones he apologized to when the Yankees didn't live up to their legendary status. The ones, as he stated in the letter he sent me, *without which there would be no need to have a Yankees baseball team.* My blood boils as I type these *noxious* words.

It angers me to hear Michael Kay talk about the sellout crowd at the new ballpark yet the camera scans patches of empty seats over the course of the game. The real crime is that corporate spectators go to the game to be wined, dined, and entertained. These bought clients have no allegiance to the Yankees. They don't care if the Yankees win or lose. They are not fans! How could Steinbrenner pretend to think that fans would want him to sell those spectacular seats to corporations while those of us who bleed pinstripes get pushed to the edges of the ballpark? We want to watch our team! We want to jump up, scream, and cheer the Yankees to another World Championship. The corporate suits won't be screaming; they'll be using their mouths to talk business and stuff themselves with fancy food. Their energy won't fill *Steinbrenner Stadium, New York* with love and passion, and I say love and passion because real fans love the New York Yankees. The Yankees are part of us and we are part of them. Their victories ours, their defeats ours—felt on a personal level that lifelong fans feel. Only real fans know what I speak of; it's a mystery to those who don't love a team. With the exception of a few men like Derek Jeter who always wanted to wear the pinstripes, players are in it for employment and, one would hope, to win. When players get traded away, they commit to a new team, because that's the cold reality of professional sports. But real fans... we're here for life! We will never be traded, and no one can tell us that our services are no longer needed. A huge part of my identity is formed around the Yankees. I spent a lifetime watching them, listening to them, reading about them, defending them, and talking about them.

I've read about competing players saying that they *hated* playing at Yankee Stadium, and that's because its fans are determined, tenacious, relentless. But a lot of that passion is gone, and it's all because of *Steinbrenner Stadium, New York.* The designers of the new place moved the bleachers away from the action, and George allowed it! They took their impassioned, insanely loyal Bleacher Creatures and moved them back, up, and farther from the action, because the real estate they had been squatting on since the Stadium was born was suddenly too damned valuable—too good, it seemed, for the Creatures! The fact that the Yankees built an empire while that real estate was occupied by bleacher seats proves it wasn't necessary to relocate them. Moving the bleachers squelched the energy of the Stadium, and the opposing players have to love it. They are no longer tormented the way they once were. The Creatures were right there in the action—part of the game, in the mix. They rallied our team to victory. Bald Vinny had to scream so loud that he sounded hoarse the last few times I was there. *Steinbrenner Stadium, New York* brought the Creatures down a few pegs; the most loyal of fans were cast aside because of money. Anyone who says the passion is the same in the new park is a liar or a fool.

We are reminded of what Yankee Stadium used to be like when we watch the Yankees play at Fenway Park, because that place is packed with rabid Red Sox fans cheering on their team. Boston could have torn down Fenway and made their base the home of corporate money, but they keep their house filled with its real fans. Fenway Park belongs to its fans the way Yankee Stadium had belonged to us. Something inside of me dies when I watch the Yankees play in Boston. It's loud and rowdy the way our house once was, but nothing was quite like East 161st & River Avenue. There was no other ballpark like ours. Yankee Stadium is one of only ten fields in the modern era that isn't named after a corporation, but the irony is that it's a ballpark built for corporations.

All other teams and their fans are glad to be done with the vacant shrine on East 161st & River Avenue, because it symbolized the dominance of the Yankees over them. I can say with near certainty that the dominance, like the old place, is gone—a thing of the past… history. The dynasty of the nineties grew the Bombers' global fan base, and everyone knows that the Yankees are the richest sports franchise in the country.

Boston charged the most for stadium seating in 2015, and the Yankees charged the second most, but Yankee Stadium holds over twelve thousand more seats than Fenway Park. The only discernible reasons for building a new ballpark lie in the two vices responsible for the corruption of both baseball and of all professional sports: greed and ego.

Donald Trump or any other quadrillionaire couldn't, or wouldn't, argue with George's philosophy, because building a new ballpark makes complete sense from a business viewpoint. Steinbrenner made it look like good business while he cemented, nearly literally, his legacy or in his case, *l-ego-cy*, into the new ballpark. He is already bronzed in it with a larger than life memorial. I can't blame his ego for that one because I assume he didn't commission it, but the enormous likeness of Steinbrenner is awkward because of its sheer size in comparison to everything else in there. Was George M. Steinbrenner more vital to Yankees history than George H. Ruth? Not now or ever—not even close. I think George might have gotten a bigger kick out of a Steinbrenner memorial created in a similar style and size as the Miller Huggins, Babe Ruth, Mickey Mantle, or Joe DiMaggio variety and placed right there among the legends; he would have been with them, not over them, for all time.

George Steinbrenner did what he did, and I have to accept his flaws with his strengths. However Hank and Hal can lend a hand and help undo some of their dad's mistakes. They can make some key changes that will reunite the fans with the team and reignite Yankee Stadium with the fervent flames of its former self.

PART 5

Settling the Score

• • •

"There is no greater misfortune than greed."

~ Tao Te Ching

• • •

Choosing Up Sides

I have a message for Yankees fans—former, disgruntled, still in the mix, or somewhere betwixt and between. You want change, right? You want to be able to bring your family to a game, sit in good seats, and be able to do that several times a year, correct? You want to be able to do that and not charge your tickets on a credit card at twenty-five percent interest. If you've had enough with the unfair prices, the corporate "owned" ballpark, and the ludicrous player salaries, then I want you to join me. You will fall into one of three categories:

One: You read the book, judge it, and forget about it.

Two: You are excited and motivated by the content, agree with most of what I've said, and determine that we have a similar mindset. You tell your friends about the book, visit my website and vent your frustrations to like-minded people all over the globe. However, after a few good venting sessions you go back to your life and continue the pattern of following the Yankees, going to games, and complaining about the subjects discussed in this book.

Three: You commit to the movement! You let the Yankees know that they are nothing without you—nothing without fans. What corporation is going to pay top-dollar advertising for a team with a shrinking fan base? If we close our wallets, we'll get the Yankees' attention, because dollars are the only language big business speaks. Reporters who cover the Big Apple sport circuit have a vehicle to say their piece in hopes to move the masses, the owners, and the players. They hope they can effect change, but they can only hope. They can't personally organize fans...

Well they could, but they would lose their credibility and possibly their job because that isn't what they are paid to do. You, on the other hand, can do something.

Specifically, we need to organize, place our demands before the powers that be, and begin our boycott until the Yankees realize that they need fans to grow their empire, and they owe us some respect—not lip service but concrete steps to right the wrongs and bring the team and its fans back together again.

Demands!

To Hank, Hal, and the rest of the Yankee brass: **We want the Stadium back!** We want a feeling of ownership in the new place; we want to feel like it's ours—not to share in monetary profits, but to have the team's profits invested in us nonetheless. We want to be able to frequent the park more often, bring our family and friends, dig in, scream, cheer, and chant our team to the World Series, and here's what it's going to take.

1) **Drop ticket prices:** There are thirty teams in Major League Baseball, and, as stated, *ad nauseam*, the Yankees are the wealthiest. In 2015 the Yankees charged their fans the second highest ticket prices. **We want the ticket prices cut in half**, which would put us just below the MLB average; the Dodgers are under the average and so are the Mets. As fans we always want the Yankees to come in first place, but this is one area where we are willing to make a concession. You could clearly afford to give us that… whether you want to or not remains to be seen.
2) **Relocate the bleachers** back to where they were at the old place, and change the section numbers back to 37 and 39 again. Respect those guys who give the Yankees so much each and every game. Of course that means you have to rip out those comfy seats in that prime real estate in right field, but that location was inhabited by the Creatures anyway, so give it back to them and let them do their

thing. The opposing teams have had it too easy. It's time to inject some of vigor into right field and put the Creatures back where they belong!

3) **Monthly fan appreciation days**: One game per month, all concessions, tickets, and parking are half off. If the vendors complain, show them the door. I'm not talking about *select sections* of the ballpark the way you sometimes sell the nose bleeds for $5.00, I'm talking about all seats—except the corporate boxes; this event is for people, not businesses. Just imagine fans thinking that you are doing something to make their day at the ball park affordable. This is called action, not lip service. This is proving to fans that you want them to bring their families to baseball games. You could call them throwback days. Maybe encourage fans to bring their old worn out Yankees apparel. It would be fun, and it would galvanize the fans and the team. You could afford to do that six times a year.

Recommendations

***Lottery:** Create a section of 10-15 box seats located near the first base line that are part of a lottery system. I borrowed the idea from the Broadway musical *Rent*, which resulted, partly, in the famed Rentheads (a group of dedicated *Rent* fans who saw the show repeatedly through its twelve-year run). Before each show, the theater auctioned off orchestra seats, arguably the best in the house, in lottery fashion, and sold them for $20 each. How awesome would that be at Yankee Stadium?

***Away games:** Fly a pair of fans to an away game, monthly. Fans would be ecstatic if they were flown to see the Yankees play in Toronto and in ballparks across the country. What could that cost, $100,000? All of this will pay off as fans' commitment to the team will increase, and you will sell more of everything. You could charge more to advertisers as your fan base rises. I've spoken to scores of people who stopped going to Yankee Stadium because they're disgusted. It's time to listen to your fans!

Teamwork

These are the demands and recommendations. If our numbers are in the thousands we will make the Yankees rethink their current business model and consider what's been addressed in these pages.

Do you think they'd notice if we boycotted specific games throughout the year? I'm not only speaking about our presence at the ballpark, I'm talking about an all-out no attending, no watching, no listening boycott. Sponsors *will* notice, and that will make the Yankees consider our case. Do you suppose the Yankees might notice if we boycotted a Yankees-Boston game or maybe even a series—maybe even boycott every Yankees-Boston series? You bet they would! Perhaps we could boycott the first game of every home stand for the first half of the season. There are many, many possibilities, so let's put our minds together and discuss the most effective strategy.

Boycotting opening day might cost the Yankees some serious profits, not to mention the negative publicity surrounding the fact that Yankees fans have had enough of the nonsense. The Yankees will hear us if we do not buy specific Yankees apparel for an entire season—no shirts, jackets, or hats, and then the next season we boycott bats, gloves, batting gloves, wrist bands, or memorabilia. We'll tell our kids why we are boycotting the Yankees, and in doing so we teach them what it means to stand up for something.

The Yankees organization is only part of the problem—the players are just as guilty.

The greedy players are a major part of this whole twisted system. I'm sorry, but you are not worth $25,000,000 a season to play baseball. Get the hell over yourselves and get back to reality. Owners with the fattest wallets and the biggest egos play each other in a fan-funded-high-stakes-free-agent poker game. Owners win some of the time, but ballplayers win every hand. As discussed, major leaguers should make a lot of money, but there's a line, and they crossed it a long time ago. If owners stop paying exorbitant salaries and fans pressure the system in the form of boycotts, ballplayers will have no choice but to stop expecting—the hard line will be drawn, and players will still make millions; it all works out.

If players aren't happy with the conditions of Major League Baseball, they could play in Japan, Mexico, the Dominican Republic, Korea, all over

Europe, and many other locations. I say goodbye and good riddance. Pro ball players could even choose another line of work if their $25,000,000 a season demands aren't met. I realize they have their standards. They could spite the owners who spurned them and teach them all a lesson by joining the masses and making $52,000-$55,000 annually—and that happens to be a twelve-month year, not a nine-month year. I'd welcome them into our world with open arms.

Hoarder

Let's take Max Scherzer for example. He's a proud one. After the 2014 season, he held out until a team submitted to his arrogant and supercilious demands. The Washington National signed Scherzer for $210,000,000 over seven years, which is roughly $30,000,000 a season. Believe it or not Scherzer rejected $144,000,000 over six years from his former team, the Detroit Tigers. Can you imagine turning down $24,000,000 a year to play baseball? How cocky can you be? Mark Lerner, principal owner of the Washington Nationals, like the other crazed owners, will keep playing that poker game. We, their pawns, are there for the purpose of fueling their fun. It reminds me of the comedy *Trading Places* when the Duke Brothers bet each other one dollar to play a silly game which ruined Louis Winthorpe's life.

**While completing the final revision of this book, I researched Max Scherzer's first year with the Nationals: he had a record of 14-12, and the Nationals didn't even make it into the postseason. Mark Scherzer still got paid all those millions—right down to the last penny!*

Stubbed

Perhaps down the road, Stub Hub needs to be boycotted as well, because people make a business out of ripping off fans. Stub Hub is a great source if a person bought tickets, can't make the game, and would be out the money if Stub Hub didn't exist. It's innovative and positive, but people abuse it. We justify paying outlandish prices for tickets bought on Stub Hub by saying that our kid deserves to see the Yankees in the postseason, or we tell ourselves that we deserve it, but this behavior only continues a destructive cycle. It's like buying stolen goods off the street. Thieves wouldn't be selling if people weren't buying. Try an experiment… Buy Yankees tickets on Stub Hub *only* if the tickets are the original price or lower. If enough people did that, I'll bet those who are capitalizing on this site will eventually go away.

What do you suppose owners are thinking when they see how much fans will pay for seats on Stub Hub? They're thinking they should raise ticket prices.

Game Time

This book began with the word *it,* attached to the phrase "It makes me sick," and it took nearly a hundred pages to explain the many aspects of that enigmatic pronoun in relation to my inner turmoil. *It* appropriately fits the bill because *it* involves a thorny web of characters, such as pride, ego, greed, fraud, contempt, loyalty, love, frustration, heartache, players, and owners. Most importantly, *it* covers a lifetime relationship between myself and my love of baseball, my love of the Bronx, my love of the Yankees, and my connection to the palpable network of Yankees fans—most of whom I've never met. These are individuals with whom I have a connection just by walking into Yankee Stadium among the crowd, or seeing one in a store wearing the interlocking NY, or even the connection that's felt when being introduced to a stranger and discovering that we both happen to be Yankees fans; this new acquaintance and I are members of a fellowship. It's why I've both given and received welt-inducing high fives and bear hugged "strangers" on humid summer nights in the bleachers after a Yankee drilled a clutch home run to tie a game in the late innings, only to know that we'll be celebrating together again when the Yankees go on to win the game—if not in this inning, the next time they're up or the time after that. I've been in this relationship years before George Steinbrenner arrived on January 3,

1973 and I will continue on for the rest of my days. I didn't write this book because I've given up on the Yankees. I've written this book because I love the Yankees, and I refuse to sit silent as the bond between the team and the fans gets ripped apart by the repulsive atmosphere of this egocentric era.

I've said all that I have to say, and I'm curious to know your thoughts. I want to know if you're with me. Are we going to just talk about it or are we're going to band together and take back Yankee Stadium? Visit me at boycotttheyankees.com. I'll see you there, and we'll plan our boycotts until the Yankees consider doing what's right by the most dedicated, committed, passionate fans on the planet; but that's a fact you already know—besides it's something you hear just about every time the Yankees talk about us.

In Solidarity,

Mike DeLucia

A man walks into a bar with a dog.
The bartender says, "You can't bring that dog in here."
"You don't understand," says the man.
"This is no regular dog, he can talk."
"Listen, pal," says the bartender.
"If that dog can talk, I'll give you a hundred bucks.
"The man puts the dog on a stool, and asks him, "What's on top of a house? "Roof!" "Right. And what's on the outside of a tree?" "Bark!" "And who's the greatest baseball player of all time?" "Ruth!" "I guess you've heard enough," says the man.
"I'll take the hundred in twenties."
The bartender is furious. "Listen, pal," he says, "get out of here before I belt you."
As soon as they're on the street, the dog turns to the man and says, "Do you think I should have said 'DiMaggio'?"

Between being a teacher, overseeing a travel club at school, family obligations, and all of the other responsibilities associated with middle-class life, it took over a year and a half to write *Boycott The Yankees.* The final revision was completed on a Saturday evening, and I was thrilled to be a click away from sending my manuscript to the publisher at the start of the workweek. As I was driving to an event that Saturday night, a memory made its way into my thoughts regarding an assignment I completed during my first year of college. About ten miles later, I realized that my book would have a supplement and the anticipated joy of hitting the "send" button was to be postponed.

I don't remember if this particular writing assignment was mentioned in the course syllabus, but I do remember the day my professor distributed the outline. The insecurities accompanying every new project caused a few people to raise their hands, and the professor called on a girl sitting next to me. The girl said that she's not an author and didn't have the ability to write a short story. Her tone indicated that she thought the assignment was unfair. The professor smiled and said she didn't have to be a published author to complete the assignment. The girl said she wouldn't know where to begin, and the professor said that she should begin with what she knows and to add aspects of her own life to enhance the narrative. The girl's protest became background noise as I considered the professor's advice. It made sense to write about what I knew, and it didn't take long for me to decide on a topic. The following story is the result of that choice.

While I'm glad the connection between *Boycott The Yankees* and the short story finally dawned on me, I wonder why it took so long, especially since both works clearly grew from the same place—my Bronx childhood and my love of baseball.

The Baseball Game

When the phone rang, I sprang to my feet and ran toward the kitchen. My older brother raced ahead and shouldered me into the living-room wall on his quest for the ringing trophy. My mother, standing in the kitchen and close to the phone, glared at Louis as he ripped the handset off the receiver—yet before he could seal the victory, he meekly forfeited his prize to Mom after noticing her deadly, blank stare and open palm.

"Hello?" Still eyeing Louis. "Yes I'm Mark DeFranco's mother. How can I help you?" A wave of nervous excitement rushed through me. "Oh hello. Mark's been looking—"

"Who is it, Mom?" I interrupted.

"Excuse me sir." Cocking her head and burning *me* with the evil eye this time. "It's your baseball coach. Can you please get me a pencil?" I rushed across the room toward the junk drawer, but Louis grabbed a pen off the kitchen counter, handed it to Mom, and smiled wryly at me. "I'm sorry for the interruption," Mom said. Using her shoulder to hold the receiver against her ear, she scribbled on a piece of paper. "Okay... Oh how nice! I'll be sure to let him know; he'll be *very* happy to hear that." My heart thumped. "Okay, got it, Monday 4:00 pm... at the main field..."

This was the moment I'd been waiting for. It was the beginning of little league season, and word was getting around the neighborhood that coaches had begun calling kids to tell them which team they were on. I looked forward to this day more than any other day of the year.

"Bye-bye now," said Mom, and she hung up the phone. Mom looked at me proudly and said, "Your coach's name is Mr. George, the name of your team is the Panthers, your first practice is Monday at 4:00 pm, and... you made it to the majors this year!" Louis shot up from the couch and bounded toward Mom.

"What? *I'm* in the majors! Mark's not old enough to be in *my* league; he's only ten!"

I said, "First of all I'm eleven, and if you're *really* good they bring you up a year early. A kid in my grade, Thomas Caraturo, made it into the majors too. He found out yesterday."

Louis said, "Well that kid's probably good. How did *you* get in? They definitely made a mistake."

Mom said, "Louis, your brother is an *excellent* ballplayer. Don't you remember that home run he hit last year?"

"Retards could hit home runs at that little field," Louis quipped.

Mom's gasp was a blend of horror and outrage. She pointed her finger at Louis, and when she spoke, she accentuated the last syllable of each word.

"Apologize, to Mark, right, now!" Louis refused, so he was sent to his room. He would have spent the rest of his life in there before he would ever apologize to me, but Mom was firm: no apology meant no dinner. Louis relented five minutes after dinner was served.

Louis hated me.

My mother said that wasn't true, but what else could she say? She was our mom. Mom was five-feet tall with thick black hair that changed with the times. At this particular period she was sporting the '60s beehive—teased and sprayed into a tower about a foot high above her head. Her girlfriend, Rosemarie, styled all of my Mom's friends' hairdos in her private beauty salon in the basement of her mother's house on Crosby Avenue in the Bronx. Mom was originally from Harlem, but after my parents were married they settled into a four-room apartment in the Throgs Neck/ Pelham Bay section of the Bronx—a small apartment building owned by my father and grandmother and filled with my aunts and uncles.

My brother Louis was thirteen years old, tall, and well-built with long black hair. He was popular in the neighborhood—partly because he was funny, but mostly because he was an exceptional athlete. I'm not sure why he hated me, but he did; he hated me for as long as I could remember. We had fistfights all the time, but it wasn't much of a contest. Louis was two and a half years older than me, and that makes a huge difference when you're a kid. No matter how hard I fought, I lost every battle. I had a few minor victories though, like this time when Louis and I were fighting over a rubber book strap. These rubber straps had metal hooks on each end that fastened to each other, and we stretched the bands around our schoolbooks and used them in place of backpacks. One day, Louis and I were fighting over one of these rubber straps, and while both of us tried to gain possession, I looked at that taut rubber stretched between us and an idea came to mind.

I released my end—

The metal hook hit Louis square in the chin, and his head snapped back as if he took a jab from Muhammad Ali. Louis had a welt on his chin for two weeks and I was punished for as many days.

I grew up in the Bronx during the late '60s and early '70s—a time when there were *always* kids hanging around the neighborhood. Where there were kids, there were games to be played and teams to be picked, but Louis would *never*, under *any* circumstances, choose me. One time Louis and his classmate Eddie "Peach Fuzz,"—the boy had a year-round crewcut—were choosing up sides for a sewer-to-sewer stickball game, and the last two kids available were Annie LaRocca, a local tomboy, and me. However, there was only one spot left to make the sides even, and my brother chose Annie. He picked a *girl* over me, which was an especially huge insult in 1969. The kids laughed, as they took their positions for the game, and I walked home sucking in quick, rapid breaths through my mouth and exhaling hot, toxic air through my nose. I tilted my head up as though I were looking at the clouds and made sure I didn't blink anything out for fear of the Neighborhood seeing. Regardless of what Mom said, Louis hated me, and he proved it every day.

The night after I was picked for my little league team, Mom, Louis, and I were eating dinner—Dad wasn't there because he put in double shifts at work and ate by himself at night. The phone rang and Mom eyeballed us back to our seats. She got up from the table and answered the phone.

"Hello? How are you, sir?" Mom listened for a while and said, "If *he* thinks so, then it's not a problem. Okay, see you Monday… bye-bye now."

Mom hung up the phone and jubilantly proclaimed, "Boys, you are on the same baseball team!"

My heart stopped!

Louis protested, "Mom call them up and tell to put me on a different team. I'm not playing with Mark—he stinks!" Mom ignored Louis and explained that our names got mixed up in the draft, but Mr. George called my coach from last year, Mr. Mooney, and Coach Mooney said that he thought I could handle it. "I knew it" said Louis. "Moon Man was probably dying to get rid of you."

Mom said, "It would do the both of you good to be playing on the same team." I'd become instantly numb. Mom continued, "Everything in life is meant to be, and mistakes aren't really mistakes at all—they are blessings in disguise."

I had been walking on air for twenty-four whole hours, because I thought I was really good at baseball. I had always been one of the better players on my team, batting between first and fourth in the lineup, but being brought up a year early meant I was special. Louis *loved* that it was a mistake, and he looked at me with a snide grin all through our mother's philosophical rant. Mom was too busy being *brilliant* to recognize the unspoken dialogue between Louis and me. Pearls of wisdom poured from her mouth, but her words floated up to the kitchen ceiling without ever touching our ears.

The first practice of the season was always a day I looked forward to, but this year I was dreading it as much as my annual torture session with Dr. Lucarelli, a man who I swear they used as a character model for the dentist in *Little Shop of Horrors*. My brother kept looking at me and laughing as we drove to the field. When my mom asked Louis why he was laughing, he said something funny happened at school, but then he would look my way and start laughing again.

Mom always drove us to the first practice so she could meet our coach and see if he looked "normal," but once he checked out we peddled our way to practice and games for most of the season. The first day of practice was a day of introductions and instructions. Our coach, Charlie George, seemed good-natured and fair. He was tall, husky, and, judging by the acne on his face, probably no more than twenty years old. He also had an odd practice of stuffing baseballs in the pockets of his jeans, which we called "dungarees" back then. The coach gathered us together, discussed the importance of coming to practice on time and good sportsmanship, and also said that *all* players would participate in every game for at least one inning. The latter was a league rule, and I was glad to hear it because, as I looked around, I realized how small I was compared to my teammates. One kid, Big John Jasinski, had legs up to his neck and was taller than the coach. Big John and Louis were teammates last season; they batted third and fourth in the lineup and were, according to Louis, feared by every pitcher in the league. My brother, naturally, made it his personal mission to inform everyone about the "mistake," and he presented it in a way that established him as a first-rate comedian and me as a perpetual punch line.

Practice sessions turned into regular-season games, and, as time went on, I realized that Louis was right about me: I stunk at baseball. I couldn't play the field or hit. When I got up to bat, it was an automatic out. I didn't play much, but when I did play I struck out every time. The ball came in so fast, I could never catch up to it; I dreaded my turn at bat, because it was another chance for me to prove to everyone that I was a spastic loser. Our hyperactive second baseman, Kevin Fitzpatrick, asked Louis if I was adopted. Louis laughed and said, "I wonder about that myself."

Even though I was a major handicap to the team, we were really good, and I hate to admit it but Louis and Big John were the best of the best. Big John was a first baseman who could stretch his long legs half way across the diamond. Ground balls hit anywhere in the infield were automatic outs because of John's extraordinary reach. Coach George affectionately called our lanky first baseman "Stretch." Louis was our speedy center fielder with a rocket arm—he could nail a runner at home plate from the deepest part of the park. Louis hit for average and led the league in home runs, as well. Maybe I was adopted after all.

While we had a couple of scrubs like me at the start of the season, I was the only one left at the end of the season because the other bench-warmers had stopped coming. When right-fielder James Landi sprained his thumb prior to the final two games, I was the only person available to fill in. We lost one of those games because I should have caught a routine fly ball, but I misjudged it. When the ball glanced off the webbing of my glove, the winning run scored, and that loss placed us into a tie for first place with the Cardinals, last year's champions.

We beat the Cardinals, or Birds as they were sometimes called, once and they beat us once, so a play-off game was scheduled to determine the league champions. The Cardinals were an obnoxious bunch of cocky kids that had screaming, hostile parents who brought everyone they knew to Cardinals' games. The Cardinals' spectators, dressed in bright red, filled their section of the stands and brought folding chairs which amped up both their presence and their intimidation factor. The Birds were the only team in the league where the players' sisters formed a cheer squad; they had makeshift uniforms, red pompoms, and performed well-choreographed cheers. The Cardinals' arrogant, gum-chewing coach, Mr. Faust, carried a beat-up rule book in his back pocket, and frequently made a spectacle of himself with his overly dramatic rants when he felt the umps were being unfair to "his boys." I loathed that team, but I also respected them because they were really good. Even though we beat them once this year, I thought they were better than we were, and I wasn't very optimistic about our upcoming contest. The championship game was set for the last Sunday in June, which ironically fell on the christening day of my brand new cousin, Kim.

Since the family had to be in two places at the same time, my parents decided that Mom would go to the christening and Dad would go to the ball field. The morning of the game, Louis and I got up, ate, and went to church. We returned home to find our uniforms cleaned, pressed, and laid out on our beds. We were running late because Fr. Mel gave a particularly long-winded homily that day. We changed, kissed Mom goodbye, and set out for the field. Dad and Louis rambled on about baseball in the front seat of our 1970, ice-blue, Dodge Dart Swinger, with a black vinyl top, while

I sat in the back seat staring out the open window watching the road to the ball field roll past.

When we pulled up in front of Wilkinson Park, I felt the beginnings of butterflies in my stomach. We were late and the park was loud and packed with people. Coach George wiped sweat from his brow with a large white towel when he saw us, and the team cheered when Louis emerged from the car. He may as well have been Mickey Mantle the way they were hooting, howling, and whistling. The only thing missing was a swarm of news reporters and autograph hounds. Louis ran ahead and was swallowed up by his overzealous teammates. Dad and I strolled down toward the field. When we got near the bleacher seats, Dad affectionately tapped the visor of my baseball cap with his fingers, winked at me, and made his way toward the mobbed stands. I headed toward the Panther's dugout with my glove slid over the handle of my Thurman Munson Louisville Slugger that I received at Bat Day.

The look of the field that afternoon was captivating. The grass was emerald green, the dirt was brown and powdery, and the freshly rolled white-chalk foul lines outlined our majestic little playing field. The sun was shining bright and it was a gorgeous day for a baseball game. I was so taken in by the view that I tripped on a rock and fell flat on my face just as I neared the dugout. If there had been nervous tension among the players, my grand entrance certainly took some of the edge off *both* teams. People bellowed all around me. I tried my best to laugh it off, but I was mortified because my dad was there. You want to impress your mom when she comes to your game, but there's something different about baseball and your dad. It's tied in somewhere between playing catch in the backyard and going to Yankee Stadium together.

I laughed my way into the dugout and slammed squarely into a wall of palpable, competitive energy—a combination of fear, adrenaline, and sweat. Coach George gave us a pep talk and sent his athletes into battle. I watched from the bench as my team trotted onto the field. The Cardinals' fans were screaming loudly and their cheerleaders began a rhythmic chant. Our pitcher, Steven "Wally" Wallace, was a tough, ugly, mean, freckle-faced, red-haired boy who cursed, smoked, and lived with his grandmother. He had a fake front tooth that he would suck in and out to reveal a grotesque gap. Wally's uniform was never pressed or clean and his hair was long, curly, and uncombed, but that kid had a golden arm. Between his physical presence, constant spitting, and slightly-wild-blistering fastball, Wally intimidated hitters. The Cardinals' coach tried to have Wally removed from our team after our last showdown, because Wally didn't legally live with his grandmother. Coach George thought it was because Wally hit one of Faust's sons, Oscar, with a fastball, and that boy writhed in pain on home plate after the ball pelted him on the hip bone. Oscar was taken out of the game, and while Oscar was back in the lineup today, I'm sure he wasn't thrilled to be facing Wally. The Cardinals were the only team to beat Wally this year, as they rallied after Oscar Faust was hit, and that did not sit well with our volatile pitcher; Wally was bent on revenge.

Both teams were determined to win the championship, and the game wore on, inning after intense inning with neither team able to score. Our pitcher may have been better than theirs, but the Cardinals were both practiced and talented. Louis got several hits and almost scored on a double by our crazed pitcher who was also good with the bat—no surprise there. Unfortunately, though, Louis got tagged out at home plate. The game was so intense, I grew weary just watching it from the bench. Coach George was screaming from the sidelines, Mr. Faust argued with the umps, and the fans were getting rowdy. When the top-half of the ninth inning began, Mr. Faust walked over to the umpire with his rulebook, and pointed to me sitting on the bench. The umpire called my coach over and, after a brief meeting, they disbursed. Coach George signaled to our right fielder, James Landi, and waved him back toward our dugout. He then told me to take the field. I'm not sure if Coach George lost track of time or he hoped that pesky little rule didn't apply to championship games, but it made no difference to me, because I did *not* want to play, and I sat there frozen.

"Let's show some hustle, Mark!" said Coach George, as he enthusiastically clapped his hands.

I felt every eye in the park staring at me as I fumbled around the dugout to find my glove. When I found it, I glanced into the stands at Dad who was clapping, whistling, and trying to cheer me on, but he had no effect. I lumbered out to my position and looked to my right at Louis in center field. He was standing there with his hands on his hips, looking at the ground, and shaking his head. I felt anxious and out of place. I *literally* prayed to God that the ball wouldn't come to me.

Oscar Faust ended the game's long stalemate by sending a Steven Wallace fastball soaring over the center field fence, and, just like that, the Cardinals were up by one run. Cardinals' fans were screaming, jumping up and down, waving posters, and throwing red confetti in the air. Wallace smoked the next two Birds on six straight pitches, but the next batter hit a high fly in my direction. I lost the ball in the sun and panicked. I tried to move but my feet were nailed to the ground. As if shot from a cannon, Louis leaped in front of me, caught the ball, stopped the bleeding at one, and possibly have saved my life—Wally was staring at me with malicious intent!

Our backs were against the wall, but the heart of our lineup was scheduled to hit. Big John Jasinski was up first, and he had tears streaming down his face, red cheeks, and a wet nose—but he wasn't sad, he was pumped! He slammed a helmet on his head, wiped his nose on his shirt sleeve, grabbed his bat, held it on both ends over his head, faced his team and screamed, "Yeahhhhh!" with flared teeth, intense eyes, and wide-opened mouth. He jogged into the batter's box. The pitcher hurled a fastball that whizzed over Big John's head, but John wasn't fazed at all. In fact, it looked as though he was more determined than ever. He roped the next pitch into right field for a clean single. Louis, replicating Big John's raised bat and toothy *roar*, followed that hit up with a single of his own that he stretched into a double. There were men on second and third with no outs, and Steven Wallace was up. Wally grabbed a bat and performed the new "scream ritual" created by Big John a few minutes earlier, but he was stopped by Coach George before turning and jogging to the batter's box. Mr. Faust called a time-out and brought in a new pitcher.

The new lefty made Wallace look like a fool on three pitches: two were nasty fast balls but the third was a slow change-up and Wallace swung so hard that the momentum caused him to topple awkwardly to the ground. Wallace threw his helmet into the fence behind home plate and the umpire ejected him from the game just as Mr. Faust was reaching for his rule book. Even if we were able to tie the score, we now had no real pitcher to start the tenth inning. The Birds pitcher made the next batter, Kevin Fitzpatrick, look just as ridiculous as Wally.

As fate would have it, I was up next. The kid who struck out every time up for the entire year was to bat with two outs in the bottom of the last inning in the game that would determine the league championship. Mr. Faust's strategy had paid off. While walking past my teammates with my Thurman Munson bat and scuffed blue helmet, I heard, "This sucks" and "Well it was a nice season." Our catcher, Michael McTigue, began violently stuffing gear into the equipment bag. Wally gripped the chain-link fence on the spectator side of our dugout; his head was down and he didn't say a word. I didn't scream "Yeah" with a bat raised over my head, I simply walked towards the batter's box to the sound of the Cardinals' cheerleaders chanting "We're number one!"

I remember looking down at my barely-broken-in cleats as I stepped up to home plate. When I got there, I took a deep breath, looked up at the pitcher and could hardly believe my eyes. The enemy had a familiar face and it belonged to Thomas Caraturo—the kid in my school who got promoted to the majors. I didn't even realize that he was pitching. We had spoken once or twice this year because we were the only two kids in my grade who made it to the majors, but Tommy's promotion was no mistake. He was big, strong, and talented. I smiled at Tommy on the pitcher's mound as I dug in and wiggled Thurman who was cocked just above my head. Tommy went into his wind-up and unleashed a fastball.

Even though the fans were chanting "We're number one!" they heard that unmistakable *crack* and watched as the ball exploded off the barrel of my bat, shot into the gap between right and center field, and rolled all the way to the fence. After I rounded first base I saw Big John step on home plate and my brother flying around third, but the Cardinal center fielder had possession of the ball and was preparing to throw home. Louis was going for the trophy and he wasn't stopping for anything. The center fielder fired the ball into the catcher's mitt ahead of Louis; Coach George screamed from the sidelines and motioned for Louis to slide. Louis dove head-first into home plate and collided with the catcher who was waiting for him.

From a cloud of brown dust and two tangled bodies came a rolling baseball. The umpire shouted "Safe!" and the game was over.

I watched Coach George and my entire team stream out of the dugout and pile on top of Louis at home plate. I was standing on second base taking it all in—a view I hadn't seen all season. Mr. Faust ran over to the umpire with his rule book, the dejected Cardinal team walked off the field, the cheerleaders consoled each other, and the Panthers' crowd jumped up and down.

As good as it felt standing on second base, I had no desire to run over and join the celebration—the distance between us felt right.

Standing behind our dugout on the opposite side of the fence was Dad. He was looking at me with a beaming smile and I smiled back at him. That was the last thing I saw before the herd of boys engulfed me with raw, youthful jubilance, the smells of baseball, and acceptance. From the center of the crowd Steven Wallace picked me up and handed me to Louis and Big John Jasinski who held me above the team. They paraded me like that all around the field. I'll never forget the proud look on my father's face as he scooped me off the tops of their shoulders, grabbed Louis, and hurried us off the field and into the car. Coach George and the rest of the Panthers waved excitedly to my brother and me as we drove away. That was the best feeling of my life!

When we arrived at the christening, Dad told everyone about his two sons' heroics. Mom looked at Louis and me with a teary smile. A moment later she handed us freshly pressed dress clothes and told us to wash and get changed. When I looked in the bathroom mirror, I saw brown dust on my forehead; I proudly left it there.

After we ate, Louis asked me if I wanted to go outside and reenact the game. I nodded and we ran out together like two little kids. When we acted out my final at bat, the Pelham Manor Catering Hall parking lot became Yankee Stadium, and Louis, clenching an air microphone, became iconic announcer Bob Sheppard.

"And now batting for James (*echo* James) Landi (*echo* Landi), Mark (*echo* Mark) DeFranco (*echo* DeFranco). The crowd goes wild… HAAARRR." We didn't have an announcer at Wilkinson Park, but I didn't mind the embellishment one bit.

For what seemed like hours Louis and I went through every inning of the game. We acted out all of the characters, like Big John Jasinski, Coach George, Mr. Faust, Oscar Faust, the umpire, Steven Wallace, the fans, Dad… and ourselves. Louis was more excited than I was. It was like he was lost in a world of fantasy. I, on the other hand, was enjoying the reality of the moment. Our long, turbulent past had been swept away with one swing of a baseball bat. My original sin of being the younger brother was washed away, and for the first time in my life, Louis spoke to me as his equal…maybe even someone he admired.

Made in the USA
Middletown, DE
07 June 2016